IN LOVE
and
IN DANGER

A Teen's Guide to Breaking Free of Abusive Relationships

Barrie Levy, M.S.W.

SEAL PRESS

In Love and In Danger
A Teen's Guide to Breaking Free of Abusive Relationships

Copyright © 1993, 1997, 2006 by Barrie Levy

Published by Seal Press
An Imprint of Avalon Publishing Group, Incorporated
1400 65th Street, Suite 250
Emeryville, CA 94608

AVALON
publishing group incorporated

9 8 7 6 5 4 3 2 1
Library of Congress Cataloging-in-Publication Data

Levy, Barrie.
In love and in danger : a teen's guide to breaking free of abusive relationships / Barry Levy.
Summary: Describes the experience of teens who have had abusive dating relationships and gives advice on how to end the cycle of abuse and forge healthy and loving, violence-free relationships.
1. Dating violence—United States—Juvenile literature. 2. Dating violence—United States—Prevention—Juvenile literature. 3. Teenage girls—United States—Abuse of—Juvenile literature.
[1. Dating violence.] I. Title.
HQ801.83.L48 1992
306.73'0835-dc20   92-41914
ISBN-13: 978-1-58005-187-3
ISBN-10: 1-58005-187-1

Cover design by Patrick David Barber
Interior design by Holly McGuire
Printed in the United States of America by Transcontinental
Distributed by Publishers Group West

The author has changed some names, places, and identifying details in this book to protect the privacy of individuals.

Contents

Introduction

This book is for teenagers who have questions about abusive dating relationships. Are you in a relationship with someone you love who is hurting you? Were you in one in the past? Do you have a friend or family member who is a teenager and is being hit? Verbally abused? Sexually abused? Do you treat someone you love abusively?

If you answered yes to any of these questions, you are not alone. There are many other young women and men who are having the same or similar problems. And there are people who can help you deal with it so you don't have to feel so alone.

This book will help you to understand what is happening to you, and to figure out if what is happening in your relationship is abuse. It will help you decide what you can do about it.

This book is for teens to share with friends, parents, family members, teachers, counselors, and others.

In the first section, you will read stories told by three girls and a mother about their experiences with dating violence. The chapters following the stories give you general information about dating violence. Many end with a summary of the information in that section and an "Exercise" page for your thoughts and feelings.

Hopefully, this book will leave you feeling encouraged and empowered to confront a very difficult teenage problem.

Speaking Out

Clarisse
"I'm attracted to bad boys"

I'm sixteen. Jon is eighteen. We were together for seven months. I met him in the parking lot where I live, where people hang out to smoke. I didn't know him at school, but after I met him I saw him at school one day. He was funny. He said we should hang out. One night at midnight, he called my cell. It was exciting to sneak out at night to hang out with him.

He loved to party. He wanted to hear about things that happened to me. When I told him I was raped a year ago, he wanted to protect me. I thought it was cool.

He kept pushing me: "Do more with me! Sneak out of your house!" It was a rush for me to sneak out. I was trying to be bad. I'm attracted to bad boys, people who are hurt, so I can help them. They need a mother. Friends think I'm like a mom. It makes me feel good, but it takes me out of my path, and I become more like them. I tried to help him all the time. He totally needed me. He was going out with another girl. He told me she was a cocaine addict, cheated on him, and he was breaking up with her. He asked me to help him get away from her. He sweet-talked. I took care of him like a little brother for two months, before I found out it wasn't true—he didn't break up with her.

He had a really bad life, and sometimes he used it to make me feel guilty. He was an orphan at six years old; no one in his family wanted him. His mom died of alcoholism.

I've been raised to listen to my parents. They're proud of me because I get straight A's. No matter how bad things get, I still bring home a good report card. I procrastinate, but it comes easy. I'm on the swim team. I'm in leadership. My parents knew nothing about Jon. They told me not to see him. They thought I went out with him for a month, and that he was gone. My dad met him once and told me that this kid would treat anyone he cared about really badly, and lie and manipulate them. He said he was trouble. Every detail of what he predicted was true!

I lived two completely different lives. My parents thought I was doing well until I started to become pale, tired, and not as happy as I used to be. They'd ask if I was doing drugs. I'd tell myself, *You should tell them. If only they knew.* But then I'd think, *They'll kill me.* I thought I was invincible; *I'll get away with this.*

He made me feel guilty. For example, if I didn't feel like sneaking out, he'd say, "So you're going to leave me alone tonight." Then if I didn't feel good about sneaking out, he'd say, "I didn't tell you to come out!"

Everything was always my fault, or I knew that it had to do with me if anything was wrong. I've always been around guys; I have guys for friends. I'm comfortable around people. He told me I couldn't see any of my friends, only girls, and he had to be with me. It was either my friends or him. The closer I was to the person, the less I could see them. I saw friends anyway, even though I'd get yelled at every time, and he'd threaten to go see another girl. And he would.

I had to be with him 24/7 so he wouldn't go out with someone else. He told my friends he'd kill them if they came near me. It was his rule—"If you're going out with me, you can't go around any other guys." I am a free-spirited girl. I tried to make him jealous. But he wanted me for himself. He'd say, "I want you to just want me." He'd talk about all the girls he'd been with

I kept thinking it was normal, what you have to go through to get a guy.

and tell stories about sex with them, to make me jealous. But it made me angry.

He was possessive and extremely jealous. He never hit me. Once he grabbed my arm, to keep me with him, and it hurt. I told him, "You won't lay a hand on me." It was the only power I had. And he didn't. But he yelled at me.

He'd say, "Your parents matter more than me!" I'd say, "Yes." He'd yell, make it worse. He started to call during the day, then every week he would call a little more, at night, then all night long. He slashed my parents' tires.

I used drugs with him. I kept thinking it was normal, what you have to go through to get a guy. This is love. A guy friend told me, "Guys don't do that!"

At times it was fun. I love being out at night. He took me to the beach at night. We went to the pier, ran up and down. It was fun. The next day he took me to the beach, and I lost my virginity. He always mentioned sex, every day. At first, he waited for it to come from me, but by then I did want to do it. He *always* wanted sex. I felt he cared. I liked it. I liked the caring. I thought things were okay; he didn't hit me. But there was always some little thing wrong. For example, I'd realize we had fun, but I hadn't seen anyone but him for a week.

Jon was still going out with the other girl. I told him he had to choose. I said, "I won't allow you to have two girls." Two weeks later, he chose me. Then I found out he was having sex all day—at 8:00 AM with the other girl, then me, then her after she got off work in the evening, then me at night.

He pushed me against his truck. I cried, "Leave me alone!"

He was with both of us every day, but he told me he wasn't, even though I could tell sometimes. I asked him, "Why can't I reach you at 1:00 PM or 6:00 PM?" I would be at his house, having sex, and at 12:30 PM he'd jump up. "I need a drink! You stay in bed." I was usually stoned. He'd say, "I'm going to Starbucks." Then he'd go to the other girl—in my heart I knew it. Then he came back. If I said anything, he'd say, "Do you think I went to see a girl? I can't believe it. You don't trust me! Am I nothing to you?" And he'd cry. I'd apologize. I felt bad. This happened for three months straight. I found out to his friends he called us his "two bitches."

Finally I called her. I couldn't stand it. I found out the truth. I told him I didn't want to see him again. He yelled at me. I told him not to pull that stuff anymore. He pushed me against his truck. I cried, "Leave me alone!" He started leaving, and I turned away. He ran after me and started bawling, telling me that he was going to kill himself, that he loved me, and he banged himself against a phone booth. I thought he was crazy. I hugged him; he had me back in his arms. I told him to let me go. He was on his knees in the street. I didn't know what I was feeling.

He often talked about killing himself. I thought he'd do it. He has scars from cuts on his arms. Now I realize he told me he'd kill himself to make me do what he wanted. Once I took a taxi to his house in the middle of the night because I thought he would kill himself. I got there and he was passed out drunk on the porch. He smirked, "You came, you little bitch!"

After I broke up with him, the next day he called as if nothing had happened at all. I told him I made myself clear: I didn't want to see him. He said, "You know that you love me." He made me feel so bad. "It's your fault I did it. You didn't trust me or love me. I had to get it somewhere else."

I broke it off. He called a lot. But I'm clear—it's over. Now he's with a new girl. She's cute, a freshman, full of herself. I don't know what to do. I'd like to talk to her, but she won't believe me, she'll think I'm crazy. I don't want people to pity me, or see me as a victim. I'm not a victim; I allowed myself to be manipulated. I made the wrong choices. I also had a lot of fun and excitement. I wish I had been given advice, that somebody would have told me that that's not the way it's supposed to be, so I could have heard it. Nobody sane behaves like that. It scares me to realize that so many people told me, but I couldn't hear it.

Julie
"I thought, *Maybe it is me that's the problem*"

I had just turned seventeen; Troy was twenty-two. I was impressionable. I thought, *He knows about so many things.* When he put me down, I took those things to heart. I met him in my junior year in high school. We were together for six months and he left a lasting imprint on my life. I was still recovering from the relationship in my freshman year in college.

My family moved away but I wanted to graduate from my old school, so I found a place with roommates—one of them was Troy. He was a friend, and offered to help. Initially everything was fine.

At first we were friends, then things changed as we began to get romantic. I grew up very sheltered and religious in a Mormon family. Troy was my first boyfriend, and our relationship escalated quickly because we lived together. Three weeks into it, the relationship was passionate, it felt good. My friends saw him as a great guy, cute, taking care of me. When the abuse started, I was incredibly vulnerable, and I had never experienced anything like it. At first, it was constant verbal abuse. He would make comments like, "Don't wear that to school, you're too fat," or "You're so ugly, you're lucky to be with me." Due to my family situation and feeling like I had no other place to go, I just took the abuse and remained grateful to him for letting me live there rent free. I did things for him, and sacrificed myself so I wouldn't make him angry. No one in my family knew. Most of my friends knew I lived with him, but initially they didn't believe I was being abused until later, when it got physical. I hid the bruises with clothing and makeup. I was a cheerleader, and usually all the girls change together in the locker room. My friends started to notice I was changing individually. One of my close friends told me I was a different person altogether. My friends didn't see the abuse until later, when it got worse.

I thought, *Maybe it is me that's the problem. Maybe I really am too fat, too ugly. I need to improve.* I started to constantly beat myself up, both mentally and physically. He would criticize what I ate, and so I began exercising a lot and eating less and less. I started taking diet pills, diuretics, and going on liquid-only diets. I developed anorexia

My friends didn't see the abuse until later, when it got worse.

and bulimia. It's still a problem today. But I'm healthier now. I recognize when I slip. I hate that I'm still letting that part of him affect me.

When I did start to lose weight, I thought he'd be happy. *Then* he told me to wear sweats to school, not show off my body. I tried to make him happy. At times it would be good, for example when I cooked him dinner. But if he had a bad day, he did things like throw dishes at me for not cleaning the house exactly the way he liked it done. He kept getting more abusive, I kept getting more withdrawn. My friend was right, I was no longer myself. I had no interest in school, cheerleading, or the volunteer work I did. I was consumed by him. My grades slipped and I was depressed.

We had a party and his friends were over. He called me over. "Get the f--- over here!" He grabbed me by the arm and dragged me over to where he wanted me. He was six foot two and powerful. His friends laughed. I was stunned.

I had never been touched like that before. The next day at cheerleading practice, I had bruise marks that I couldn't hide, so not only did I change my clothes separately, I also made excuses for the bruises. More and more of my friends started noticing I was acting different, but most of them couldn't put their finger on why.

I couldn't afford a car, so I depended on Troy for rides to and from school and work. I would often end up taking the bus, which would anger him because he claimed he was there to pick me up but just late. He was nice to me when he wanted me to do things for him. Living with him and his roommate, I also began to get involved with drugs.

The first time we had sex it was terrible. It was intense, he liked it rough. Whenever I would beg him to stop, he would somehow get off on it. I remember just closing my eyes, imagining I was somewhere else and crying silently. I hated having sex. I had sex with him so he wouldn't hit me. He sometimes used objects. I thought it was his penis, but then I saw he wasn't in me. He used a small souvenir baseball bat or a cucumber. I never used birth control. He wouldn't wear a condom.

I told him I was pregnant when I found out at five weeks. He said, "It's okay. We'll handle it." He was calm. I was relieved that he didn't get angry. That night he took his baseball bat and rammed it into me. I miscarried that night on the bathroom floor. I passed out when I saw the pool of blood, and woke up in a puddle of vomit and blood and in incredible pain. I was trembling. As he was cleaning up the mess, he said, "I told you I'd take care of it." I was in shock. I couldn't believe it. He cleaned me up and took me to a clinic. I was passed out in the car. Now it's 75 percent likely that I can't ever get pregnant. For a while I had night terrors. I used to have traumatic recurring dreams about the miscarriage and the unborn baby.

I talked to my brother's girlfriend and told her everything two weeks after the miscarriage. She told my brother to do something. Initially he was disgusted, but he came to the apartment and told me, "Pack your stuff. We're leaving." I packed everything I could carry in one suitcase and left everything else there. Those things didn't matter. I got out. My brother saw the bruises, but at my request didn't tell my mom or my family about my living with Troy.

My brother went back to Troy's house with his friends. They sabotaged the apartment, and his friends were supposed to help him beat up Troy, but my cousin said they ended up keeping him from killing Troy. My brother was *very* angry. He threatened to report Troy for statutory rape. Troy knew he could prove it because I still had bruises. He moved out of state, and I haven't heard from him since. I never had an urge to call him or go back.

That was the first time in my life that I thought I wouldn't go to college. I loved to learn, and I loved school. That year I went from being an A-plus student to getting all D's. But I had good support at school from friends, teachers, and an amazing counselor. I took my classes over. With help from others, I was able to pick myself back up and put the pieces of my world back together. I'm graduating from college this June. I feel I can conquer anything now.

I never really loved Troy, nor do I believe that he ever really loved me. I have had two relationships since then. I didn't have sex for three years after I broke up with him. I caged myself because I didn't want anyone to have as much power over me as Troy did. After three years, I realized that this thinking allowed him to still rule my life. I finally released him when I had sex with a friend. Since then I've been okay with sex. My current boyfriend is supportive and understanding, like my best friend. He cried when I finally told him a little about what happened. I realize now I'm not stupid for having been with Troy, and I have come to truly embrace the fact that what doesn't kill you only makes you stronger. I'm okay now. I *can* have a healthy relationship. For a while I believed I was damaged goods, since I probably can't have a baby.

People will care, but you have to care enough about yourself to seek help.

I pushed away even good guys, believing they wouldn't want me.

I saw a therapist who helped me find ways to empower myself, to not let this hold me back. Group therapy is great for adolescent girls. It was key for me, not only to get over the trauma, but also to value relationships with friends. I've triumphed in so many ways in my life, and while I struggled many years to come to terms with what happened to me, today I can say that I'm honestly glad I was faced with this challenge because I am that much stronger and determined because of it. However, I can't say I did it alone. I feel immensely grateful for all the social support I received, and I know it was the generosity and love of others that helped me get through this.

For other individuals out there reading this story, and possibly even experiencing something similar, all I can offer you is hope. Hope that you can help someone like me or hope that you too will survive the abuse. Reach out to someone if you need help or try to be someone who can be reached. People will care, but you have to care enough about yourself to seek help. It's taken me over five years to overcome a six-month relationship with my abuser, so I know it's not easy and that rising above the abuse will take time. Your power and your strength can only shine during challenges.

Adaliz
"I thought things would change"

I was twelve years old when I met Richard. I had lots of friends, but I never had a boyfriend before then. Richard was very popular. He was quiet, a sweetheart. I was madly in love with him. (Now I look back, and I realize it was junior high school—and the excitement of my first boyfriend.) My parents didn't allow me to see him because I was too young. So I told them I stopped seeing him, but I didn't. I started hiding things from them.

Richard and I started acting really serious, as if we were older. He started getting possessive. I wanted to enroll in the drill team, but he said no, those girls were all sluts. He made me feel guilty, so I didn't enroll. That was the beginning of him telling me what to do and making me feel guilty and bad about everything.

I remember the first time he hit me. I met him at the corner to walk to school. I had on a light blouse with a slip under it. He thought you could see through it. I told him if my mother let me leave the house with it on, there was nothing wrong with it. He got mad and called me a bitch. He socked me in the face and knocked me down. I couldn't go home. What was I gonna tell my mom? So, crying, I went to school with Richard, and when we got there I changed into my gym clothes and wore those all day. I never wore that blouse again because I was afraid of him.

From that day on, he told me how to dress and who to talk to. If I did something "wrong"(which means that made him jealous), I would fix it and do what he asked me to. I didn't want to make him mad. I think now, *If I could have put my foot down then, would he have stopped?* Maybe. A lot of girls are like me, and do what I did. They're scared and don't want to lose the guy.

Our problem was always his jealousy. I wasn't going out with anyone, but he always thought I was looking at someone, or he thought my clothes were too tight, or that I walked too sexy. How, at the age of thirteen, could he even think of those things?

What hurt me the most were his mean words. I wasn't used to the kind of names he called me. My parents never allowed that kind of language. I cried a lot. I walked looking down. I'd ditch school a lot, and, although I made sure I passed, I was falling behind. I was miserable. I'd tell him he was hurting me verbally. I'd try to break up with him, then he'd cry and say, "I'm sorry. Don't leave me. I'll stop hitting you." I'd believe him, because I didn't want to leave him; I wanted him to change.

When I was in eighth grade, Richard was a grade ahead of me, and we were in separate schools. He would ditch school so he could walk me to school and pick me up. He had to make sure I wasn't doing anything. He'd find out from his friends if I was talking to someone, and we'd get in a big argument. He'd call me disgusting names and make me cry. He'd hit me, push me, sock me in the stomach and in the head. He was smart. He knew not to leave me with bruises that showed.

He told me about problems his parents had. He used to jump on his father to stop him from hitting his mother. He said he'd never hit me like his father hit his mom. Then when he hit me, he'd say he didn't mean to, and turn it around so that it was my fault: "If you just didn't do those things, I wouldn't hit you." In other words, I shouldn't get him mad, or provoke him to hit me.

After a while, my parents found out I was still seeing him. My friends would tell their mothers, who would tell my mom. My sister would also tell my mom. She would question me, but I would say no. I was close to my father, and he tried to talk to me. My parents started taking me to school. They did everything they could to stop me from seeing him. The more they kept me away from him, the more I wanted to be with him. I ask myself now, *Why did I let that go on?*

The more they kept me away from him, the more I wanted to be with him.

When I went into ninth grade, I went to the same school as Richard. My parents hunted everywhere for a different school for me. The other schools wouldn't allow the transfer. I was happy—I wanted to be in the same school as him. As our relationship continued, and after we started having sex, the violence was worse and worse. He didn't like anything I wore or did. His power to control me made him feel good. He was always pushing me to have sex. One time, we were already in school, and he wanted me to ditch because he wanted to have sex. He wanted to go to his house because his parents weren't home. I said no, I didn't want to. He dragged me by the hair, socking me. We were near a field at school where students and a teacher were planting a garden. The teacher called the narcs [school police]. They handcuffed and arrested him. I wanted to go back to school, but they made me go with them, and they called my parents. My dad came to school and told them to press charges. My dad convinced the principal to get the school near where he works to admit me there. The school permitted it because of the situation, on the condition that I would do good work in school.

Now my parents knew about the abuse. So my dad would take me and pick me up every day. I couldn't go anywhere. I couldn't make calls. My parents answered the phone, and wouldn't let me talk to Richard if he called. I thought my dad was a mean person. Now I realize that he didn't want it to come out like it did. He didn't want me to be hurt.

All I wanted was to be with Richard. So I ran away from home to be with him, and lived with him at his aunt and uncle's house for one and a half months. But his jealousy, mean talk, and hitting got worse. I thought being with him would make me happy, but I was miserable. After one incident when he accused me of "fucking" his uncle, I couldn't take it anymore, and I went home to my parents.

But I continued to see him, even though I didn't want to live with him (I was fourteen). By the time I went home, I was pregnant. I hid it for six months. I thought my parents were going to kick me out or something. They are very religious, Jehovah's Witnesses. We never talked about abortion or adoption. I kept the baby. But even then they didn't allow me to see Richard.

Richard beat me worse when I was pregnant. He always aimed for my stomach and the back of my head. It was always because he thought I was looking at a guy, or some guy looked at me. Two weeks before my daughter was due, I went with my sister to see her boyfriend. Richard was there. Right away, he wanted to have sex. I told him no because I didn't feel good, and all those people were there.

He got mad and pushed me so that I fell straight back. I had so much pain I screamed. My sister was so angry. Richard said he was sorry, he was under so much stress because he couldn't see me.

The next day I had the baby. He came to see me that day and while he was there the doctor came in to check me. He got mad and yelled, "He had to touch you?" I said, "He's a doctor!"

The second time I was pregnant, I also had the baby early because he beat me. We got married while I was pregnant with our second daughter, when I was sixteen. We lived with my parents. I continued in high school—in eleventh grade. I wanted to graduate with my class.

Richard went to college to study computers and worked at night. We didn't see each other that much, and when we did, we fought a lot. Living with my parents was full of stress. Many times I left the house because I got fed up with him hitting me.

When I was around his mother, she would get mad at me: I shouldn't provoke her son to hit me. Everything was my fault. She didn't like my parents. Richard's mom used to say to my mom, "Why are you taking care of your daughter? She's not a virgin anymore." She would tell my mom I'm a slut. My mom had more class than to say anything. My father would talk to Richard, open the Bible and say, this is the way to treat your wife. Sometimes I wished he would beat Richard up and tell him to stop beating me. Now I'm glad my dad's not that kind of man.

I thought when we got married things would change, and he would stop beating me. I thought, "God, why should he hit me anymore? He can see me all the time. Everything

I do, he'll see. He'll trust me." But he got worse. I was his now; he thought he owned me. Over the next four years, the violence got worse.

When we were in church, he pinched me and called me "bitch!" when men were around. He hit me whenever he thought another man looked at me. He attacked my womanhood; he often pinched me and socked me on my breasts, and kicked me between my legs. He dragged me down the steps by my hair. He slammed my hand in the front door. He kicked me with steel-toed boots after knocking me on the ground.

I was so careful to never give him a reason to get mad and beat me.

Several times when he hit me, I called the cops. My parents now knew because they could hear him socking me. I'd deny it and say I fell. My daughters would cry when they saw him hitting me. Sometimes they cried even when someone was playing, or my sister tickled me.

I tried everything. I'd throw clothes away he didn't like. I never even thought of having an affair. I was a good wife. He never had to ask me to wash his clothes or to take care of the girls or cook meals. Everything was always done. I was so careful to never give him a reason to get mad and beat me.

Two years ago, after our son was born, things got worse again. Richard socked me in the face and broke my nose—and something snapped inside me. I didn't care anymore. I didn't plan to stop loving him. But something clicked, and I said, "I am not gonna go through this no more and that's it." I realized that this guy's not going to stop at anything. I left Richard.

He wouldn't face the fact that I left him because of the violence. He was sure I left him for another man. Richard still wants to get back together. He says he's changed. He has promised so many times he'd never hit me again. I don't believe him. Right now, it scares me to think of being with another man. It took me a lot of courage to get up and leave him. Since we separated, I am still trying to understand why he did that to me. I am twenty-one, and I have a lot I want to do with my life. I am stronger now, and I want to talk to other girls like me, so they won't stay with a boyfriend who abuses them like Richard abused me.

Terrie
"She was a prisoner"

I met Bobbie's new boyfriend, Josh, for the first time at her sixteenth birthday party. He was nineteen, and he came with a group of girls and boys who were Bobbie's new friends. They were different from her old friends. She didn't tell me much about them, but I heard their names more and more during the next few months, and I saw less and less of her old friends.

Bobbie was a straight-A student. She won a journalism award when she was a junior in high school. She was a talented ice-skater, and attended acting classes twice a week at a well-known theater group. By the time she was fourteen, she was already beautiful. She always took great pride in her appearance, putting on makeup before going to school every day, and dressing carefully. She was very outgoing and funny, always laughing and joking. She was loving and eager to please. She got along well with everyone, and never gave us any reason to worry about her. That was before she met Josh.

At first, when Josh came to the house, he dressed nicely and he was polite. I had just had a baby, and he was friendly, and proposed that we all do things together.

My husband and I began to become uncomfortable about Bobbie's relationship with Josh because he was so different from her. For example, he was not interested in school, and he wasn't as active as she was. We decided to "see how it goes." We were afraid that if we pressured her or told her what to do, she would do the opposite. We figured she would get tired of him.

Then Josh started coming around looking awful. He'd come over barefoot, with no shirt and filthy hair, with an open beer can in his hand. He would go right to Bobbie's bedroom and shut the door.

I would tell her not to shut the door, and that Josh couldn't come over looking the way he did. He was disrespectful. Bobbie would get upset. She started getting critical of everything going on in the family. Her manner became completely different. When I asked her about her old friends, there was always a problem with *them:* This one was too busy, that one had a new boyfriend she didn't like. Her friends stopped calling or coming around.

I found out she was skipping school when I started getting calls from the school counselor. The first time, I was shocked to find out she hadn't been in school for a whole week, and that she had given the school a note with my forged signature. I'd ask her about it, and she'd overreact, sobbing and denying it. I realized later that she was hanging out with Josh rather than going to school.

Her appearance started changing. She stopped wearing makeup. She went out with dirty hair and in sweats and torn sneakers. She started losing weight. She was already small, and during that year she went from 118 to 90 pounds. She had colds and sore throats constantly.

I thought she was trying to get attention because she was jealous of the baby. I really didn't see all of these changes as signs that Josh was hurting her, and that they were using drugs. I finally realized he was hurting her when I got a call one day from Josh's mother. She asked me, "Do you know where Bobbie is?" She told me that Josh had torn apart her house with lead pipes and, with a gun, had taken Bobbie in her car and disappeared. His mother had called the police, and they had an all points bulletin out. I was terrified. An hour later, I got a call from Bobbie, from a 7-Eleven thirty miles away, saying, "Come get me!" My husband went to get her. The side of her car was bashed in. Bobbie said, "We had a fight, and Josh drove his truck into the side of the car."

Josh was picked up by the police a few days later and was jailed for a week. Bobbie was at home, falling apart. When he got out of jail, he showed up at our house at one o'clock in the morning. He wanted money from Bobbie so he could leave town. I wouldn't let Bobbie leave the house. She gave him some money, and he left.

My husband and I decided the next day to send her away to boarding school. She cried, relieved. She was glad he was gone, and glad she had parents who could do this for her. We told the school to call us if this guy ever came around.

Four months later, we got a call from the school. Bobbie had left with Josh. She called us from a resort one hundred miles from here, and told us in a mean and nasty way that was not like her that she wasn't going back to school. I got in my car and found her and took her back to school. This happened four or five times, until we enrolled her in public school and she returned home because she just wouldn't go to the boarding school.

The problems started again, and it was clear to us that she was so involved with Josh and with drugs that she defied whatever we did to stop it. People started coming around to our house at one or two o'clock in the morning looking for drugs, and finally we told her, "You can't do drugs here." When she left, I thought she'd be back in a couple of days. She was gone for a year. She called a few days later and told me where she was living with Josh. She had dropped out of school.

During that year, I called the police many times, I went to get Bobbie and brought her home many times, and I kept trying to get her the help she needed to get off drugs. Each time, Josh would come to get her, and she would go back with him.

I kept hoping that her ties to her family would be strong enough to help her get through all this.

But Bobbie and I did stay in touch. I did everything I could to keep her in our family. I kept hoping that her ties to her family would be strong enough to help her get through all this, and come home.

On Mother's Day, I picked her up to bring her home for dinner. One eye was black and blue, her nose was swollen and had been bleeding, and she had a swollen lip. She said she had been in a fight with a girl. I didn't believe her, but she stuck to her story. Finally I said, "If you're getting hurt, I want you to get medical care. I'll pay for it. Just get yourself to a good place to get the care you need."

A short time later, I got a call late at night from the hospital emergency room. She had a split lip, swollen eyes, and was dehydrated from drugs. The nurse said that her boyfriend had dropped her off, and she was crying for him. "I want Josh." She said, "I told him to take me here because you said I should, but he was mad. Please call him. I have to be with him. I can't leave him!" I took her home, but she disappeared again.

I became obsessed about her. All I thought about was if she'd be alive the next day. I'd have to call her at six o'clock in the morning to see if she was alive.

Sometimes when I called her, she wasn't there. Once, she wasn't there for three or four days, so I went over to look around. An older woman rented a house in back of theirs. I asked her if she had seen Bobbie. She asked me in to sit down. "Are you a Christian woman?" she asked. "All you can do is pray for her. Josh took her away in his truck. He has guns." I asked her to call me when Bobbie came back, or whenever Bobbie was in trouble. She was frightened, but finally she agreed.

That morning at one o'clock in the morning she called. Bobbie's back, and it's quiet. After that, she called me many times.

Bobbie's life with Josh was a nightmare. He was intensely jealous. He wouldn't let her see her friends or her family. He wouldn't let her come over for Sunday dinners. She would say she couldn't come unless he could come too.

She would visit sometimes when he would drop her off for an hour and then come back and pick her up. He'd wait outside in his truck. Or she would call me when he wasn't home and ask me to help her with something, or say, "I want to see you, but I only have an hour." Anyplace we went, she'd have to rush to get back when he said or when he got home.

On her seventeenth birthday, I took her out for lunch, and we met at a restaurant. He dropped her off, she came in, rushed, and said, "Let's eat fast, because he's coming at 1:30." She'd be so frightened, and worried about not doing what he said. When we'd go shopping for clothes, she restricted herself and wouldn't buy things she liked. She could never wear a bikini, only a one-piece bathing suit. "He'd never let me wear that," she'd say in fear.

He wouldn't let her have things she needed or money to buy them. She called once because she needed Tampax, and he wouldn't let her go out, or give her money to buy some. A couple of times when I saw her she hadn't eaten in a few days.

Josh controlled everything. He gave her things to his friends. She wasn't allowed to call me. She warned me not to call her, saying she'd call me when he was gone. She was a prisoner.

He'd burn her clothes—because he'd get mad at how she looked, or because I got them for her. He slit a leather jacket I got her for her birthday with his knife.

If he got mad at her, he beat her, knocked her out, or threw her out. Once the old woman called me because Bobbie was outside crying hysterically in a rainstorm. It was pouring outside. He had beaten her and thrown her outside and locked her out. She was drenched and cold, and he wouldn't let her back in the house.

"Come now!" she said. "I don't know if she's dead or alive!"

Bobbie was always trying to save Josh. "He doesn't have a family," she'd say. Or, "He never had Christmas." Or, "He never had books." She believed that if only she could do enough for him, or give him all the things *she* had, he'd change—because he'd love it so much, he'd become more like her.

Sometimes she wouldn't see me because she couldn't stand for me to see her the way she was: beaten, a prisoner. She told me later that those days when I couldn't find her, she was staying away from me. "I wanted to come home, but I didn't want my mom to see me like that." She was also afraid for us. Josh threatened to hurt the baby, or to do something violent to all of us. So she stayed away to keep him away from her family.

I kept trying to get her away from him. I'd get her into drug treatment programs, and she'd stay for a few days. Then Josh would come to get her and she'd leave with him. We spent so much money trying to get her help. It ripped our family apart. I was always afraid she was going to die.

One day I was about to leave to meet her for lunch, and I got a call from the woman in the back house. "Come now!" she said. "I don't know if she's dead or alive! There was a huge fight. She's lying on the front lawn." I raced over.

Bobbie was unconscious on the grass. Her stuff was thrown out there—her clothes, her radio. I shook her and woke her up. The side of her head was one huge bruise. I took her to the emergency room. After kicking her all over, Josh had held a plant in a clay pot over her head as she lay on the ground, and he dropped it. She rolled away in time so that it caught the side of her head. If it had hit her where he aimed it, she would have been killed. The police came; she filed charges. When they took photographs of her at the police station, she was bruised everywhere—her legs, her back, everywhere.

She was in the hospital for a few days, then Bobbie said she was ready. I took her to my sister's in Massachusetts, three thousand miles away. She stayed a month, and when she came home, she was herself again. She had her old friends over to the house. She got into counseling, and she attended a support group for battered women. She enrolled in the community college.

One day, Josh met her in the parking lot at school after

her class. She came home from school, and went out that night in her old sweats. I knew Josh was back. She stayed out all night. She called the next morning. "Mom, come get me. I left while he was sleeping. I'm never going back. I just had to see what it was like, to know for sure that I'm never going back to that." I was furious. I told her she had to get out of town, that he'd always find her. Twenty-four hours later, the day before her eighteenth birthday, I took her to the airport, and she went to live with my sister in Massachusetts.

She worked for a while, then decided to go to college. She started dating a boy who was a little younger than she was, and he invited her to his high school prom. They went to football games, and she did all of the things she had missed out on in high school.

Bobbie went to school in Massachusetts for three years. Josh has shown up a couple of times. My husband and I have called the police, and, the last time, when Josh apologized to us for all of the trouble he has put us through, we told him that if that meant anything he would never come here again. Bobbie said to me recently, "I hope that someday I won't be scared of Josh!" She said, "The hook of violence is so intense. I'll never love anyone the way I loved him. And it was so overwhelming, I can't talk about it without crying."

2 Facts About Dating Violence

Now that you have read the stories told by Clarisse, Julie, Adaliz, and Terrie at the beginning of this book, you may be having all kinds of intense feelings. Did you see yourself, your friend, or someone you care about in these stories? Did you realize how badly it hurts to be insulted, hit, or sexually tormented by someone who is supposed to care? Did you realize that love and romance can turn into a prison? It is painfully hard to see these things.

It took a lot of courage for you to pick up this book. It might be hard for you to read. You might see yourself in the girls or guys who talk about their experiences. It could be painful to find out that it is real, and that it really is happening to you or someone you care about.

Reading this book is an important step. Maybe it's a beginning for you—to change your life, and your feelings about yourself. Maybe it's a beginning that will help you reach out to someone you care about.

Please note that we sometimes refer to the abuser as "he," because it is most common for the abusive person to be male, but sometimes the abuser is a young woman. So as you read this book, keep in mind that the people you are reading about are in intimate relationships where a guy abuses his girlfriend, or a girl abuses her boyfriend, or a guy abuses his boyfriend, or a girl abuses her girlfriend.

> *The first time it happened, I was about fourteen and my boyfriend was sixteen. He saw me hug my brother in the hall at school, but he didn't know it was my brother because [my boyfriend and I had] just started dating. He dragged me out of school, behind a store, and just beat me up—literally. He said if anyone asked me what happened, to tell them I got into a fight with someone, but not to dare tell anyone he hit me.*
>
> —Anonymous, 17

You may think you are the only one this is happening to. But that's not true. Many teenagers have problems with violence in a relationship with a boyfriend or girlfriend. In fact, young women ages sixteen to twenty-four are the most vulnerable to relationship violence.[1] Several surveys asked teens if they had been hit or sexually assaulted by someone they were dating or seeing. The surveys showed that about one in three high school students has been or will be involved in an abusive relationship. And 40 percent of teenage girls ages fourteen to seventeen said they knew someone their age who had been hit or beaten by a boyfriend.[2]

Dating violence is *serious*. Teen girls and young women are four times more likely to be victims of sexual assault than females of other ages, and the majority of those crimes are committed by someone the girl knows.[3] Every abusive relationship has the possibility of ending in murder. The number of young women murdered by a boyfriend is alarmingly high. According to the FBI, one out of every three women murdered in the United States is killed by an intimate partner (husband or boyfriend),[4] and 20 percent of female homicide victims are between fifteen and twenty-four years old.[5] Even if the abuser doesn't intend to kill his girlfriend, a hard shove or threats with a weapon can "accidentally" kill.

Dating violence happens everywhere and to all kinds of people. There is no particular culture or community in which it occurs. This means that it happens in big cities and in small farming towns. It happens in wealthy neighborhoods and in housing projects. It happens in every culture and ethnic group. It happens in gay as well as straight relationships. It happens to teens who have babies and those who do not. Although it is more likely to happen to couples who live together, it often happens to those who do not.

As with all kinds of abuse, it is most common for young women to be the victims and for the violent partner to be male. However, young women are also the perpetrators of and young men are also victimized by dating violence.[6] The majority of dating violence occurs when the relationship is serious or steady. In several studies, young men were more violent as they began to see themselves as part of a couple.[7] Some abusers become more violent when they think the relationship is going to end, or after their girlfriend or boyfriend does break up with them.

Do you believe that violence is a normal part of dating? Do you believe that hitting and jealousy are signs of love? Many teens believe this, even though it is not true.[8]

Notes

1. "Bureau of Justice Special Report: Intimate Partner Violence," May 2000.
2. Ibid. Cited on The Alabama Coalition Against Domestic Violence Website, www.acadv.org/dating.html.
3. V. I. Rickert and C. M. Wiemann, "Date Rape Among Adolescents and Young Adults." *Journal of Pediatric and Adolescent Gynecology,* November 1998.
4. Bureau of Justice Statistics, "Homicide Trends in the U.S." FBI Supplementary Homicide Reports, 1976–2002. Cited on the Family Violence Law Center website, www.fvlc.org.
5. Ibid.
6. D. Sugarman and G. Hotaling (1991). "Dating Violence: A Review of Contextual and Risk Factors." In B. Levy, ed., *Dating Violence: Young Women in Danger.* Emeryville, California: Seal Press, 1991, 1998.
7. J. Henton, R. Cate, J. Koval, S. Lloyd, and S. Christopher, "Romance and Violence in Dating Relationships." *Journal of Family Issues,* September 1983.
8. D. Sugarman and G. Hotaling, ibid.

3 What Is Dating Violence?

*I've been with Carlos since I was thirteen. He used to choke
me, do awful things. He used to make me feel that no one
else would want me. I felt I better stay with him. He scared
me. Sometimes we would be driving somewhere, and all of
a sudden he would take off with me in the car and drive
to a parking place. Then he'd hit me because of something
wrong I said. I was afraid of everything I said, afraid to
say the wrong thing.*

—Consuela, 19

In a violent dating relationship, a person repeatedly
threatens to or actually acts in a way that physically,
sexually, or verbally injures his or her boyfriend or girlfriend. It does not just happen once, but happens again and
again. It is *not* the same as getting angry or having fights.
In a violent dating relationship, one person is afraid of and
intimidated by the other.

Being abused by someone you love means being mis-
treated by him or her. This may be emotional or physical
or sexual, or all three.

Emotional Abuse

Eighteen-year-old Sandy said:

> *I was insulted, accused of crazy things, humiliated, and had my mind twisted. I was constantly criticized and called names. I was put down, no, verbally attacked for things that were not a problem the day before. I was blamed for everything that went wrong. Often, I had no idea what was wrong.*

Sandy knew she was being hurt. She realized later that it has a name: emotional abuse.

Emotional abuse can be very confusing for teens. It is very confusing to be told you are worthless by the person who expresses such great love for you. One fourteen-year-old girl, who didn't want us to use her name, said:

> *I figured maybe I did wear too much makeup, or maybe my skirt was too short, or maybe I really was a "stupid fucking bitch." Maybe I did look like a whore, or maybe I shouldn't have gone out with my friend. Since I loved him, I figured,* Why would he lie to me? He loves me.

Jealousy and possessiveness are emotionally abusive. Abusers' jealousy and possessiveness give them control over the person they love. For example, thirteen-year-old Salina described how the excitement of romance became controlling:

> *We spent all our time together. It was wonderful at first, but it became obsessive. I was either with him or talking to him*

on the phone. He became more and more jealous. At one point, I even had to be on the phone with him when I went to sleep so that he knew I was at home at night. I was allowed to talk to only two people at school—both were girls—and he had his friends watch me to make sure I was obedient.

The abuser's jealousy and suspiciousness lead to accusations and intense questioning or interrogations. Jealousy leads to verbal harassment about everything you do or say—in the name of love. Jill was convinced that David loved her. She said:

He often showed it through his extreme jealousy and possessiveness. I couldn't talk to another boy. . . . He resented my girlfriends and my family. He said, "All we need is each other." If he chose to go out with his friends or not bother to call me, I was supposed to sit at home and wait for him to call. If I wasn't there, I was interrogated over and over about where I was, who I talked to, even what I wore. The hassle wasn't worth it. I became more and more isolated, more dependent on David, and afraid of David's temper if I didn't do what he wanted.

Abusers' anger can make it too frightening for their boyfriend or girlfriend to do anything that will set them off. Sixteen-year-old Jim's girlfriend was terrified of his raging fits when he was jealous. He never hit her. He yelled at her, called her names, interrogated her for hours about everything she said or did with anybody. Later, after seeing a counselor, Jim said, "After a while, I got what I wanted: complete control over my girlfriend. Power."

When asked, "What are some of the ways you have been *emotionally abused?*" teens answered:

- yelled at
- had money stolen
- constantly blamed for partner's own faults
- verbally harassed
- called names
- constantly accused of flirting or having sex with others
- repeatedly interrogated
- publicly humiliated
- had treasured possessions broken
- labeled "stupid" or "crazy"

Another way an abuser gets control with emotional abuse is by making a girlfriend or boyfriend feel crazy and doubt himself or herself. This could happen to you if you are threatened that your secrets or even lies about you will be revealed in school. If you are in a gay or lesbian relationship, your abuser may threaten to tell everyone at school that you are gay or lesbian. Or your abuser may say one thing and do the opposite. Or say or do something, and then deny it, telling you that you are crazy or stupid.

Abusers also use emotional abuse to get control when they keep their girlfriend or boyfriend isolated. This could happen to you if you are being told that your friends and your family are no good, or if your abuser has a fit of rage every time you see a friend, or accuses you of betrayal if you talk about him or her to anyone else. Often it seems that your abuser sees your family, especially your parents, as enemies. If so, you may feel that if you talk to your parents you are being disloyal to your abuser.

Your things may have been thrown at you or destroyed. Thirteen-year-old Melanie repeatedly threatened her boyfriend, Brian, to try to control him. She verbally attacked him, or threw things when she didn't like something he did. For example, she broke Brian's portable music player when she picked it up and threw it against the wall across the room. She blew up because Brian was at the movies with his sister when she called earlier that day and wanted him to come over.

Emotional abuse destroys your independence. It makes you feel terrible about yourself. You begin to feel totally dependent on your abuser and that "no one else will ever want you." Felicia, eighteen, said:

> *He beat me, but, you know, it was the verbal abuse that killed me the most. I just felt like I was no good, I was trash, the things he used to say to me . . . that I would never get another boyfriend in my life, that I'm a bitch, a whore.*

Physical Abuse

Physical abuse includes pushing, hitting, slapping, kicking, beating with a fist, choking, and attacking with an object or a weapon.

If you have been physically abused, you may have been restrained until you were bruised, or pulled by the hair. Sixteen-year-old Dawn grabbed her sixteen-year-old

> **When asked, "What are some of the ways you have been *physically abused?*" teens answered:**
>
> - scratched
> - choked
> - hair pulled
> - cut with knife
> - arm held so tight it bruised
> - head hit against wall
> - slapped or punched in face, arm
> - arm twisted
> - hit with object
> - dumped out of car
> - burned

girlfriend, Cathy, by the arm and wouldn't let her leave. Later, Cathy had huge bruises on her arm. Fourteen-year-old Tawnya's boyfriend, Todd, who was fifteen, yanked her head back by her hair in the hall at school after he saw her talking to a classmate.

Physical abuse is not a onetime incident. It is a pattern in the relationship, and happens again and again. Each time you are hit, it is worse than the time before.

Physical abuse is used to control you, to restrict you, to scare you.

Sexual Abuse

Sexual abuse is mistreatment by sexual acts, demands, or insults.

You may have been violently forced to have sex. One fourteen-year-old girl described her experience:

I was lying on the sofa crying, and he would stand over me, call me disgusting names, masturbate, and ejaculate all over me. [Sometimes] he would tie me up. Nothing felt good to me. All I ever did was lie there. I hated it, but usually I had no choice. Not once did sex even feel remotely good.

You may not have been violently forced to have sex, but coerced or manipulated into having sex. What does "coerced" mean? Being coerced means being afraid to say no to sex. For example, you may not say no if you are afraid of being rejected, or if you are afraid of being hit. It means being manipulated so that you feel so bad about yourself or so afraid that you go along with sex when you don't want to. You may have been coerced to have sex by your boyfriend's threats to leave you, or by being made to feel inadequate or ugly.

Sixteen-year-old Luis would tell Kim (who was thirteen) that she looked fat, that she was ugly, but he put up with her. Luis wanted to have intercourse, and though she really liked him, she didn't want to have sex with him. He said it would be too much for him to put up with her if she didn't. She felt ashamed, and was afraid she'd lose him. So she didn't stop him when he pushed her onto the bed and forced himself inside her, without caring about her feelings. The same thing happened again and again, and Kim felt more and more ashamed, and didn't realize until later that she was being sexually abused by coercion.

> When asked, "What are some of the ways you have been *sexually abused?*" teens answered:
>
> - called sexual names
> - wanted sex after hitting
> - made me walk home nude
> - always wanted sex, mad when I didn't want to
> - forced sex
> - forced me to do "disgusting" sex acts
> - bit, pinched breast
> - acted indifferent
> - threatened to get a new woman
> - raped
> - slapped, pinched to get his way
> - forced me to have sex without protection

Maybe you have refused to have sex or to do certain sexual acts, but have been ignored. Seventeen-year-old Suzanne got sick at the thought of oral sex, and even though she said no, eighteen-year-old Brad would push her head down on him and wouldn't let her up until she "did it."

You may have been forced to have sex with others, or to watch your boyfriend or girlfriend have sex with someone else. You may have been humiliated or insulted sexually, so that you feel ashamed, or you feel that there is something wrong with you. Nineteen-year-old John would point to guys on the street and tell seventeen-year-old Manny how good the other guys looked, and how ugly he was, and how Manny didn't give him good enough sex. He'd say to him, in front of their friends, that he wanted to do it with this guy or that guy, because Manny was no good.

You may have been forced to have sex without protection from pregnancy or HIV/AIDS. Joan, who was sixteen, said:

> *I listened to everything Jeff said when it came to sex, because he was the first guy I was with. Whenever I asked him to use a condom, he refused. He said it "ruined his pleasure." He told me in this mean way that I couldn't satisfy him, and made me feel ugly. I'd cry. He'd lie and say he had an AIDS test and I shouldn't worry. Or he'd say that his doctor told him he can't have children, so we didn't need birth control. I realized it wasn't true when I got pregnant. I had an abortion, which was the hardest thing I have ever had to do.*

Exercise

Use this blank page to write down any of the ways you think your boyfriend or girlfriend has been *emotionally* or *verbally abusive* to you. Write the ways you think they have been *physically abusive.* Write down the ways you think they have been *sexually abusive.* Write about how you feel after reading this section.

4 How Can You Tell if Your Relationship Is Abusive?

For Victims

I had no idea I was being abused. Then my mother showed me a book, and I read other girls' stories of their abuse. I realized what they were saying was happening to me. Before that I kept justifying everything he did to me. It changed my thinking from, What did I do wrong? *to,* I don't deserve to be treated like this.

—Sandra, 19

Many victims don't recognize that they are being abused. They don't realize how they have gradually changed because of the abuse. Are you a victim of dating violence? Answer the questions below. If you answer yes to two or more of them, you are in an abusive relationship, or your relationship is likely to become abusive.

Are You a Victim of Dating Violence?

- Are you frightened of your boyfriend's or girlfriend's temper?
- Are you afraid to disagree with him or her?
- Do you find yourself apologizing to yourself or others for your boyfriend's or girlfriend's behavior when you are treated badly?
- Have you been frightened by his or her violence toward others?
- Have you been hit, kicked, shoved, or had things thrown at you?
- Do you avoid seeing friends or family because of his or her jealousy?
- Have you been forced to have sex?
- Have you been afraid to say no to sex?
- Are you forced to justify everything you do, every place you go, and every person you see to avoid his or her temper?
- Have you been wrongly and repeatedly accused of flirting or having sex with others?
- Are you unable to go out, get a job, or go to school without his or her permission?
- Have you become secretive, ashamed, or hostile to your parents because of this relationship?

For Abusers

Getting locked up for my violence has helped me to confront my problem. Before that I threatened my girlfriend verbally, and I smashed her hand into a wall. I pushed, grabbed, shook her, and put a gun to her head.

—Allen, 18

If you are emotionally or verbally abusive, you may believe that you are also a victim. You may believe that others cause your problems, and cause your violence. The result is that you don't recognize that you have a problem that only you can change. Answer the questions below. If you answer yes to two or more of these, then you are an abuser.

Are You an Abuser?

- Are you extremely jealous and possessive?
- Do you have an explosive temper?
- Do you consistently ridicule, criticize, or insult your girlfriend or boyfriend?
- Do you become violent when you drink and/or use drugs?
- Have you broken your girlfriend's or boyfriend's things or thrown things at her or him?
- Have you hit, pushed, kicked, or otherwise injured her or him when you were angry?
- Have you threatened to hurt or kill the person you're dating or someone close to her or him?
- Have you forced her or him to have sex, or used intimidation?

continued on next page

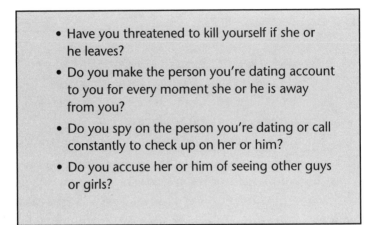

- Have you threatened to kill yourself if she or he leaves?
- Do you make the person you're dating account to you for every moment she or he is away from you?
- Do you spy on the person you're dating or call constantly to check up on her or him?
- Do you accuse her or him of seeing other guys or girls?

5 Patterns of Love, Violence, and Fear

One small disagreement would lead to another. . . . [It] would build to a crescendo, which always ended with . . . Mike's violence. Then the storm would clear, and we would make up passionately and be happy for days or weeks until the next storm started to build.

—Marge, 18

If you are in a violent relationship, it will get worse unless something changes—unless the person who is violent takes active steps to change, or unless the victim leaves. You may have noticed that there is a pattern, a cycle in your relationship. Abusers seem to be like two different people: loving some of the time, and cruel some of the time. If you are in an abusive relationship, you may experience a tense cycle alternating between explosive, abusive behavior and "making up." Some call this pattern "traumatic bonding," or the "hostage syndrome." It may cause you to go back and forth, in and out of the relationship, feeling a push/pull between intense closeness (or bonding) and intense fear or anger.

Dana and Jason are both sixteen years old and have been dating for eight months. When Jason is tense, he becomes more and more temperamental, edgy, critical, and explosive. He blows up over little things, throws things, and constantly criticizes Dana. He "punishes" her for "mistakes." He blames her for anything he feels is wrong—no matter what she does. Jason is jealous and possessive. He accuses Dana of dressing too sexy, or flirting, or having sex with others. He calls her constantly to see where she is—or to make sure she doesn't go anywhere.

Sometimes, Dana thinks Jason's demands are flattering. They seem to prove his love. She knows she is important to him. But Dana has become more and more afraid of doing something that will trigger his temper. In response to Jason's anger, Dana becomes very careful. She is afraid to do anything she believes will make Jason become violent. She tries to keep the peace, to please him. She disconnects from her own feelings and becomes completely focused on him, watching everything he does, says, and feels. When he wants to know where she's been, she tries to tell him the truth. Then she tries to tell him what she thinks he wants to hear. When he gets mad at what she says, she tries to explain.

After a while she realizes it doesn't matter what she says. Jason twists whatever she says so that he just gets angrier and angrier. When she tries to calm him down or humor him, or gets quiet just to get it over with, he keeps building his anger up to an explosion point. Sometimes it just ends as suddenly as it started, or he says he wouldn't get this way if he knew she loved him. Then he wants to have sex. When he is like that, sex isn't fun, because Jason is trying to prove something, and he's rough with her.

He calms down a little, but the tension is still there. And Dana keeps watching him, trying to avoid fights. She becomes nervous and on edge. She gets terrible stomachaches; her doctor thinks she is developing an ulcer. Sometimes she gets sick. She is usually a happy person, full of energy, but when the tension between her and Jason gets bad, she becomes withdrawn and depressed. She watches Jason closely and forgets to take care of herself, so she goes to school in old or dirty clothes. She gets so distracted with worry about Jason that she can't concentrate in school, and although she is usually a good student, she forgets her assignments and fails exams.

Sometimes the tension results in an "explosion" or escalates to a violent outburst. Jason's anger builds, and he stops trying to cool off. He lets it go and lashes out at Dana. He calls her names, hits her, and won't let her get away from him. Then suddenly, his tension is released. It's over (until the next time). Afterward, he feels sorry and is afraid that Dana will leave him. He has given her a black eye and bruises, and when he sees how he has hurt her, he cries and begs her to forgive him.

Dana tries to get away from Jason before he explodes, and sometimes she can, but other times she can't. It is a relief for her when it is over. But it also makes her angry. No matter what she does, Jason hurts her. A couple of times, after he has beaten her up, she has broken up with him. Before this, she believed and hoped this wouldn't happen again. She ignored what she knew deep down—that it would. Now that he has hurt her again, she doesn't feel so bonded with him and instead feels hurt, angry, and scared.

Jason does everything he can to get her back in love

with him. Jason is apologetic, romantic, and passionate. He promises to change and never hurt her again. Dana is unhappy and wants to get away from him. But he is so much like his old self, and he feels so bad, she remembers the things she loves about him when he is not abusive. She knows that he loves her, and that he needs her. This is what keeps the couple together. Dana can't stand feeling angry and afraid of him.

They become loving again, and Jason is not so tense. He is fun to be with again. Dana feels relieved, her energy is high again, and she feels better. Jason doesn't feel so easily irritated and jealous, and doesn't seem to twist everything Dana says or does anymore. They go to their special places and enjoy their time together.

They both find excuses for his "blow up"—his unhappy childhood, his trouble in school, her failure to keep him happy. They may even think that his violence was justified or deserved. They deny the fact that the violence is Jason's problem. He doesn't control *himself* and *his* temper. They both begin to believe that the violence was a "misunderstanding" and won't happen again. . . .

* * *

Traumatic bonding is the development of strong emotional ties between two people, with one person sometimes manipulating, yelling, harassing, beating, threatening, abusing, or intimidating the other, and sometimes being kind, loving, and/or caring. Dee Graham and Edna Rawlings are psychologists who describe how this works. When you are hurt by the abuse, you feel frightened that your physical or emotional survival is threatened, that you will never be okay or safe. This is what it feels like to be traumatized.

As a result of being traumatized, you need comfort and protection. You might be isolated from others, for example if you feel you can't tell your family or friends what is happening. Then you might turn to the person who abuses you for the love and protection you need. If the abuser is loving or kind, you might become hopeful that he will change, and not feel angry at him for terrifying you before.

So you become bonded to the loving and kind side of the abuser and work to keep him happy, becoming sensitive to his moods and needs, hoping he won't hurt you. You might try to think and feel whatever he thinks and feels, taking on his views and forgetting your own. You might see your parents and others the way the person who abuses you does—as being against your relationship, being your enemy, trying to come between you and your great love.

Your own feelings, needs, and opinions, especially your anger or fear, get in the way of your doing what you must do to be safe, so you gradually give up having feelings or views of your own. But at times, you *do* feel angry or afraid, and you try to get away from the relationship. So you go back and forth, leaving and getting back together. Sometimes you feel a special bond, and you want to take care of and protect him. And sometimes you feel like you won't survive if you stay with him. These different feelings make it hard to leave, and keep the relationship going through intensely emotional ups and downs.

Exercise

Use this blank page to write about how you are feeling or to make notes for yourself.

6 Why Do Guys Abuse Their Girlfriends?

My mom's boyfriend hit me to teach me to be tough. My mom used to hit me, and when I got angry, I'd hit in any kind of situation. I enjoyed intimidating people.

—Ray, 18

It is hard to explain why people might be cruel or violent to someone they love. There is no single explanation for it. There are several factors that contribute to violence in relationships.

Jealousy

Many high school and college students say that jealousy is the major cause of dating violence. Although it is based on insecurity, teens often think jealousy is a sign of love. The abuser says, "I love you so much I can't stand for you to have other friends. I want you all to myself." A girlfriend or boyfriend feels flattered by this proof of love.

But the girlfriend or boyfriend may ignore the way jealousy leads the abuser to restrict and control, and to hit and be violent. What starts out as romance and "special" love becomes a prison for the person who is loved. Love becomes a prison when an abusive boyfriend says to his girlfriend, "I want you all to myself," and then has jealous, angry explosions when his girlfriend sees her friends or does something she wants to do for herself. Because she is afraid, the abuser's girlfriend tries to avoid the abuser's bad temper and violence. So, gradually, she stops doing things or seeing people that are important to her. She becomes more isolated, and more dependent on the abuser as the only person in her life. And the abuser becomes *more* jealous and violent, *not* less. That is because he discovers that his jealousy gives him an excuse to control the person he loves, by keeping her intimidated, frightened, and dependent on him. (This also applies to girls who control their boyfriend with jealousy, and to same-sex relationships as well.)

In fact, jealousy does *not* really come from loving feelings. People are jealous because they are insecure about themselves, and they are afraid they won't be loved. Because they are insecure, they use their jealousy to dominate and control the person they love.

Using Violence to Assert Power

In our society, teenagers can learn mistaken ideas of what is normal in a relationship from what they see in movies, television, and advertising. They see many situations in which a strong person or group maintains power by using violence to control people who are less powerful. For example, they see bigger or older kids bully smaller or younger kids. They see governments use armies or bombs when they have a conflict. They see women treated badly in the movies or on TV. Then they see that people think it's romantic or funny or not serious. They may see adults they know using violence to show they have power. So they assume that maintaining power with violence is normal.

Not Treating Women with Respect

Young men often believe it is their right to abuse a woman. They may mistakenly believe that men should dominate and control women, and that women are passive, stupid, and obligated to please men.

There is a lot of peer pressure on guys to be sexually active, so sometimes they are sexually aggressive with girls. Guys feel it is their role to be dominant and to control their girlfriend's activities and behavior.

Guys get approval from their friends for being "the boss," for keeping their girlfriend "in line" by pushing her around, or ignoring her when she says no to sex. They may be afraid they won't look "man enough" if they don't behave this way.

Girls feel pressured to do what their boyfriend wants them to do, even if it hurts them. Girls often learn to be dependent on their boyfriend. They learn to put their boyfriend first, and not have anything important in their lives apart from the relationship. They are judgmental and critical of girls who are not seeing one special guy. A girl feels peer pressure to be in a relationship even if it is not good for her.

Girls feel pressured to have sex when they don't want to. A girl may blame herself if her boyfriend makes her have sex in spite of her saying no. The pressure comes from mistaken ideas about sex and about relationships. For example, teenagers often believe that if a guy takes a girl out, she is "obligated" to have sex with him, even if she doesn't want to. Many teenagers believe that a guy is justified in raping a girl if he is turned on by her or if he has spent money on her. Once a girl agrees to have sex with her boyfriend, she may believe that she doesn't have the right to say no, or to change her mind or not want to do particular sex acts, or she may believe she doesn't have the right to say no on another date—as if he "owns" her. Or she may be afraid that she will lose her "reputation," and be seen as a "slut" by other teens if she doesn't agree to his "ownership" of her.

These beliefs contribute to dating violence.

Violence During Childhood

Young men who were abused as children or who saw their mothers being abused are more likely to abuse their girlfriends, wives, or children. They have learned from their abusive parent to blame others for their problems. They have learned to release their tension by exploding and losing their temper, no matter who gets hurt. They have not learned other ways to handle their problems and feelings. They have not learned to treat women with respect.

Difficulty Handling Insecurity or Anger

Guys or girls who are violent with their girlfriend or boyfriend have trouble handling their insecurities and fears. They are afraid the person they are with will leave them, so they have trouble trusting. They also have trouble controlling their anger. They blame their girlfriend or boyfriend when they lose their temper. They don't know how to communicate or to talk about their feelings. They don't empathize or understand how the person they're dating can feel afraid and upset when they get angry and treat her or him badly.

When asked why they abused their girlfriends, guys answered:

- I'd get jealous. I'd get crazy if she looked at anyone else. If she dressed pretty, the way I like, I'd be out of my mind because I'd think everybody's looking at her.
- My dad beat up on my mom.
- I had a hard time trusting anyone, especially girls.
- I kept thinking she would leave me and I'd go crazy. I wouldn't want her to get to me like that. So I wouldn't let her do anything without my permission.
- I felt powerless as a child in my family, and I wanted power, so I took it—in my gang and with my girlfriend.
- I was jealous.
- I have bad anger flashes. I can't control my anger.
- I felt bad about myself. I get violent if I can't trust.
- I had a problem with alcohol and drugs.
- I was a victim of emotional and physical abuse, and I have a hot temper.
- I felt I had to be tough, to be a man. I thought my girlfriend was pushing me around, controlling me.
- I get violent when I drink, but I didn't stop drinking.

Alcohol and Drugs

Many teenagers who have experienced violence say that drinking and using drugs make it worse. They don't *cause* violence. But drinking or using drugs allows a person to let down inhibitions and become violent.

For example, a guy gets drunk at a party and after the party takes his girlfriend home and verbally and physically attacks her. At the party, he is able to decide *not* to beat up other people. He has saved it for his girlfriend. If he had decided not to drink, he might have been able to decide not to beat up his girlfriend, too. So he uses his drinking as an excuse to be violent toward his girlfriend.

The abuse of alcohol and drugs is often a dangerous way of avoiding personal problems.

7 Romantic, Nurturing, and Addictive Love

He had to have my attention whenever he wanted it. He expected me to wait around for him when he was busy. He called me in the middle of the night if he wanted to tell me something. One day I found out he was cheating on me, and that he lied to me about a lot of things. He told me it was my fault. That night, I was begging him to give me a second chance. I asked him what I could do to make him want me. I was terrified of losing him.

—Sandra, 19

You meet each other, you like each other, you find each other exciting and fun. You fall in love. Love can be nurturing, romantic, or addictive. What kind of love do you have?

Romantic Love

Almost all relationships start with **romantic love.** In romantic love, everything seems perfect, as if you have found *the one* person who is just right for you. You can only see the good things about each other. Even things you don't like you think of as positive. For example, later you might think she is "selfish," but at the peak of romance, she is not selfish, just "forgetful." Later, you might think he is "domineering" or "possessive," but at the peak of romance, he is "devoted" and "loving."

Romantic love is thrilling, exciting, passionate. You forget about everyone else in the world but your new love. You do special things together, buy each other things, write passionate letters, talk on the phone for hours.

As you spend more time together and get to know one another, your new relationship starts to fit into your usual way of life. You see your friends again. You focus on school again. You survive your first disagreement and begin to realize that sometimes you see things differently. You find out that there are things you don't like about each other.

Some couples decide not to continue seeing each other, because they realize that this isn't what they want after all, and they really aren't a good match. Couples that do continue seeing each other find ways to work out their differences, and to love each other after the romance of the beginning wears off.

As the romantic love gradually changes, and it always does, love becomes either **nurturing** or **addictive.** There can still be romance and passion between you, but it is part, not all, of what you have together.

As you are reading this, you may be thinking, *Romantic love is so great! That's the kind of love I want!* Romantic love is exciting at the beginning, but it is **nurturing love** that lasts a long time and makes a couple feel good being together.

Nurturing Love

If you and your boyfriend or girlfriend have **nurturing love** for each other, you both wish for the other to grow and to be happy. You wish for the other to be everything he or she is capable of being. You encourage each other to have friends and to enjoy activities that you do separately as well as those you do together. You support each other to do well in school or at work. You feel safe to express your feelings. If you have an argument, neither of you is afraid of the other. You are comfortable being yourself.

If one of you wants time alone, the other can accept it. What if one of you wants to end a relationship based on nurturing love, and the other is not ready? The one being left feels sad, upset, and may have a difficult time for a while. But being left, you do not feel self-destructive, as if your life is over.

Mary and Steve met at a friend's party, and within a week, they were seeing each other every day. They laughed a lot. Everything they did together seemed special. They were in love. For three weeks, they passed notes to each other in school, walked home together, did homework and watched TV together, talked on the phone from the time they each went to their own house until they went to sleep at night. When they had been together almost a month, Mary told Steve that she was going out with a group of her friends on Friday night. She had also been missing pep team practice to be with him, and she didn't want to be kicked out. Steve had wanted to see Mary Friday night, but he told her, "Go and enjoy yourself. Friends are important." When she told him about pep team practice, he was relieved, because he had been missing his pickup basketball games since he met Mary. They continued to see each other a lot, but they gradually got back into the groove of their usual activities and friends.

They had a big fight when Steve didn't want to take Mary's little sister with them one Saturday night. They both felt terrible and were afraid they were going to break up over it. Mary thought Steve didn't understand about being in a big family because he wasn't in one. Although Steve continued to hate it when Mary wanted to bring any of her sisters along on their dates, they worked it out. Every now and then (not every week), they took one of her sisters out, and brought her home in the middle of the evening so they still had time alone together. They disagreed about other things too. But they were crazy about each other, and as time passed, they liked each other more and more. Their relationship made the change from **romantic** to **nurturing** love.

Addictive Love

Addictive love can lead to trouble. You are "addicted" if one or both of you believe you cannot live without the other. Feeling intensely romantic after you first meet, you want to be together every minute. Then gradually you feel more desperate to be together, as if you need each other, and are terrified of being alone. You find yourself doing things that aren't good for you so that you can be together. Anything your boyfriend or girlfriend does apart from you threatens you, as if you are going to lose him or her if you aren't together constantly.

Guys may hide feelings like this from their girlfriends, because they think it isn't manly to feel you "need" a girl. So a guy expresses these needs by being controlling and critical. For example, he might demand that his girlfriend have nothing in her life but him. Or he might tell her that she is not good enough as a woman or as a girlfriend, and make her feel dependent on him.

Not every addictive relationship is abusive. But relationships like this are more at risk for abuse. If you are abusive, you take advantage of your girlfriend's or boyfriend's addictive need for you, and use force to control her or him. If you have addictive love for your girlfriend (or boyfriend), you will do anything to keep her (or him) from leaving, including making her (or him) afraid to leave.

If you are the abused girlfriend or boyfriend, your addiction can lead you to ignore or excuse the violence. You may be afraid he or she will leave you, and become afraid to be alone. If you don't leave the relationship or if you don't object to the way you are being treated, your abuser may think he or she has permission to be more abusive. You become a handy target when your abuser is upset with anything in his or her life.

Debbie and Lenny lived a block apart, but didn't really know each other because they went to different schools. But one day they were hanging out with kids in the neighborhood, and they were flirting and having a good time. Lenny asked Debbie out, and before he knew it, Debbie was calling him constantly, giving him poems and talking about their future together.

Lenny thought Debbie was the most beautiful and exciting girl he had ever met, but he was a little scared because things were happening so fast. He told Debbie he wanted to slow down a little, go out together with friends, and have some time apart from each other so they could keep up in

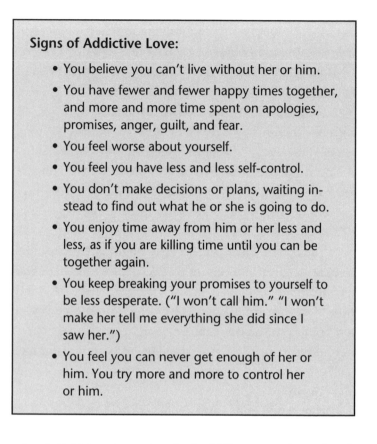

Signs of Addictive Love:

- You believe you can't live without her or him.
- You have fewer and fewer happy times together, and more and more time spent on apologies, promises, anger, guilt, and fear.
- You feel worse about yourself.
- You feel you have less and less self-control.
- You don't make decisions or plans, waiting instead to find out what he or she is going to do.
- You enjoy time away from him or her less and less, as if you are killing time until you can be together again.
- You keep breaking your promises to yourself to be less desperate. ("I won't call him." "I won't make her tell me everything she did since I saw her.")
- You feel you can never get enough of her or him. You try more and more to control her or him.

school. Debbie got upset and asked if he was trying to break up with her. When he said, "Not at all!" she said she couldn't see why they ever had to be apart.

When Lenny made plans to play ball with his friends, Debbie called him six times before he left his house and after he got home. She needed to know that he missed her, because she didn't think she could live without him. Lenny started feeling overwhelmed, although he loved her, and he told her they should not see each other for a few days. He got the scare of his life when Debbie called in the middle of the next night saying she was going to kill herself because he didn't love her anymore.

Lenny and Debbie's relationship made the transition from **romantic** to **addictive** love.

Exercise

Use this blank page to write about your relationship. Is your love addictive? Write about your feelings or make notes for yourself.

8 The Scars Caused by Dating Violence

She was worried all the time, and she lost a lot of weight, not like she was fat or anything, and she didn't see a lot of her old friends. Her other friends and I drifted away for a while.

—Rosa, 18

I was blond, green-eyed, and 130 pounds. I competed in gymnastics—until I quit because he wanted to spend more time with me. After two years with Andy, I weighed over 250 pounds. I never left my house. My education had been suffering. I had one girlfriend with whom I spoke, and that was it.

—Anonymous, 14

I started feeling real inadequate. My grades went down dramatically. I missed class a lot because I felt sick— stomach stuff, real nervous stuff. . . . It was probably a deep depression, but I started feeling sleepy all the time. All I wanted to do was stay in bed. It just seemed like everything just kept going down, down, down.

—Anonymous, 19

I f you are being abused, or if you were abused in the past, you are a *survivor*. You are reading this book. You are asking questions. You have gotten through moments of feeling like you might not live, or of feeling hopeless and totally bad about yourself. Yet you keep finding hope and strength. You find ways to fight to keep yourself going, to protect and take care of yourself.

Sometimes you might think that this is no big deal. You might forget about your strength and think of yourself as weak. But you must be strong to be here reading this book today. And you are helping yourself to begin to heal.

Verbal insults and name-calling, hitting, being forced or coerced to have sex when you don't want to: These hurt. They cause long-lasting physical and emotional effects. You may be feeling some of the effects of the violence in your relationship. Do you have any of the following?

Physical Scars
Do you have scars from injuries? Do you have bruises or broken bones? Do you have stitches? Do you have a permanent disability from the physical abuse, such as hearing loss or paralysis?

Neglected Appearance
To avoid triggering your boyfriend's or girlfriend's jealousy, do or did you neglect your appearance? Do you dress in baggy, unattractive clothes? Are you afraid to look attractive? If you have been sexually abused, do you hate yourself and your body? Have you gained or lost a lot of weight because of the stress and nervousness caused by being abused?

Shame

Do you feel ashamed, as if there is something terribly wrong with you because this happened to you? Do you blame yourself for the abuse? Do you now question yourself, your decisions, your abilities, your appearance—and you didn't before the abusive relationship?

Fear

Are you fearful or nervous a lot of the time? Do you get a stomachache when you hear people arguing? Do you panic when you see someone who reminds you of your abuser? Do you have nightmares or flashbacks about the violent things that were done to you? Are you terrified of making mistakes or saying the wrong thing—no matter who you are with?

Do you find yourself thinking about your abusive boyfriend or girlfriend all the time, because you have a habit of watching him or her closely?

If you have broken up with your abuser, are you afraid that he or she will try to hurt you? Has he or she threatened to in the past ("If you ever leave . . ."), or is he or she still threatening or harassing you?

Isolation

Are you isolated and alone? Have you lost your friendships and your closeness to your family because your boyfriend or girlfriend demanded it? Did you start to feel ashamed, and withdraw even more from your family and friends? Are you afraid to see your friends now, because you are afraid they won't believe you? Are you afraid that they think you caused the abuse? Are you afraid your friends won't understand about the closeness and intense bond that kept you together even though your boyfriend or girlfriend was violent?

Protective Feelings

Do you feel that you protect your relationship with your abuser, even when it is not good for you to do so? Do you feel paranoid at times, not trusting anyone, or afraid of people interfering?

Depression

Are you depressed? If you are depressed, you might answer yes to the following questions. Do you feel as if you have no energy, or you're tired all the time? Are you tearful, or do your emotions go up and down too much? Do you sleep too much, or have trouble sleeping? Has your eating changed and have you gained or lost a lot of weight without wanting to? Do you have trouble thinking about the future? Do you think about yourself and your life as worthless? Do you think about dying or killing yourself?

Exercise

Use this blank page to write about your scars or, if you are an abuser, the scars you have caused your girlfriend or boyfriend.

9 Healing from Abuse

I f you are feeling any of the effects of being in a violent relationship that are mentioned in this book, or if you are feeling others that are not mentioned here, *you need time and support to heal*. You have been hurt—physically and emotionally. It takes time to feel like yourself again. It takes support from parents and family members, from friends, from counselors, from others who have had similar experiences. It takes being around people who are *not* abusive so that you can feel the difference, and feel safe to be yourself again. You can use the strength you have used to survive in the relationship to do things that make you feel good about yourself again, and to heal. When you are out of the relationship, you can focus that strength on yourself (rather than on dealing with your abuser).

Even though violence may have some long-lasting effects, you *can* heal from them. You *can* feel like yourself again, and you can feel happy and trusting again. It takes courage—like the courage it has taken for you to read this book. Say to yourself, "I have courage. I *will* heal and be happy again."

10 Break Up or Stay?

My reasons for staying with him, I see, were very stupid reasons. I found myself hanging on to the boyfriend I had met at first, the nice one, instead of realizing that this might be a different person now—a violent one, a drug addict. This one beat me up. I just wanted to hang on to the nice one.

—Catherine, 17

Mostly I was afraid of what she would do. My biggest thought was that she was going to change and that I was strong and good enough that I could help her change.

—Chris, 18

I started trying to break up with him. But he would come to me crying, "I love you. I'll never hurt you again." When I'd see him cry, I'd remember the softness and gentleness he could show. It would give me hope that we could work it out. I'd leave him and go back. When [his crying] didn't work, he started threatening to hurt me and my friends and my mom. It even got to the point where he threatened to commit suicide.

—Salina, 13

Being in an abusive relationship is overwhelming. You wake up in the morning saying to yourself, *This is the last time I'm going to take this!* Then you think, *But I don't want to be alone!* Or you think, *My baby won't have his father!* And some mornings you wake up and say, *I love him! I'm not going to take this, but I'm not going to break up with him either!*

Why It Is Hard to Decide

Victims usually try to find some way of getting away from the violence without having to break up. You may be clear that you want the violence to stop. No one *chooses* to be in a violent relationship. No one likes to be called names, accused of awful things, hit, or raped. But you may not be at all clear about wanting the relationship to end. Making a decision to change your life is challenging. It is empowering. It is also frightening, and hard to do. It takes a lot of courage to change your life.

There are so many reasons you might be afraid to end the violent relationship. Are you afraid of being alone? Are you afraid because your boyfriend or girlfriend becomes more threatening or violent when you talk about breaking up? Are you afraid you will never find someone to love you again? If your relationship has been sexual, are you afraid you will be seen as a "slut"? Are you overwhelmed by how hard it would be to stay away from him or her, or to convince him or her to stay away from you? Do you feel you don't deserve (or won't get) anything better? Of course you are afraid to leave! You are afraid it will be as hard to leave as it is to stay and be hurt.

While it may *feel* just as hard to leave as it is to stay, it

When asked why they stayed and didn't get out of a violent relationship right away, girls answered:

- I really loved him (when he was not being violent) and hoped he would change.
- I felt I was the only one who understood him—he needed me. I felt I could help him.
- He'd cry and promise not to do it again. I believed it.
- My friends think he's great, and, ashamed to admit we had problems, I kept trying to make things work.
- I was afraid of him because he threatened to hurt or kill me, or other guys I might go out with.
- I felt lucky to have him and believed that no one else would want to be with me; I was convinced that I was ugly, stupid.
- We go to the same school. I was pressured by his friends, like I was doing something terrible to him when I told him I wanted to break up.
- I believed that everything would be fine when his problems were solved; for example, when he didn't have pressure from parents or school.
- I believed that the violence would stop when we lived together or got married, because then he would trust me.
- I have tried to break up, but he harassed me or became so depressed he scared me, so I tried to keep things calm until the "right" time.
- I had a baby with him. How could I break up with the father of my kid?

is far more dangerous to stay. It will hurt you more in the long run to stay and be repeatedly abused.

You deserve to be treated lovingly—and respectfully. It is *your* life, and you deserve to be in charge of it. You are strong, and courageous—look what you have already been through!

What Has Led Girls to Decide to Break Up?

Teens who break up with their abusive boyfriends or girlfriends have different reasons for finally making the decision. Often they decide to leave several times before they actually break it off permanently.

What led them to decide to break up?

- **Finally believing they didn't deserve to be treated badly**

   It made a difference to hear from my friends and family members (my sisters, my brother, my parents) and others that I didn't deserve to be treated badly.

   When the police and the principal at school and the courts responded to what was happening to me, and said that this was a serious crime, I realized how badly I was being hurt.

   When I heard it enough times, I finally believed it: What was happening to me was wrong, I was being emotionally and physically hurt, and I didn't deserve it.

- **Realizing the violence was getting worse**

  I realized it wasn't going to get better, that the abuse was getting worse.

  Something snapped for me when Richard broke my nose. Deep inside I knew that if he broke my nose, something worse would be next.

  I suddenly stopped hoping he would change. And when I realized that he won't change, I couldn't love him anymore.

- **Realizing they were losing too much**

  All of a sudden I realized that I was losing too much.

  I realized that my son was being damaged by seeing his mother get hit.

  I was planning to go to college, and I had hopes for the future. But I realized that my boyfriend wasn't allowing me to have hopes and plans because of his jealousy.

  There were lots of things to enjoy that I had missed because of the abusive relationship. I wanted the freedom to do things my friends do, that other teens do. I wanted to meet new people, go places, participate at school, do things with friends and with my sisters and brothers.

- **Hitting bottom**

  I realized that I was being dragged down. I hit bottom, and I decided to survive—and that meant leaving my boyfriend.

  I looked at myself, and realized I was becoming something I hated. I had to leave my boyfriend, and I had to stop doing drugs and drinking.

- **Realizing they couldn't stop the violence**

  I saw my boyfriend hitting and being mean to a girl he was seeing when he was cheating on me. I realized that it wasn't me, or anything I did. There wasn't anything special or bad about me that made him violent. Then I realized I had to get away from his violence—nothing I could do would ever change it.

- **Having support from family and friends**

  Friends and family who were encouraging and supportive helped me decide to leave.

  My friends confronted my abuser.

  My family helped me to protect myself from my abuser. They listened.

- **Getting new, hopeful perspectives**

  I read a story in the newspaper about a girl who was abused by her boyfriend, and I knew that was what was happening to me. I realized I could get out of this. I felt hopeful.

  In a class I took, we did reading about women and girls and relationships, and we discussed things that helped me understand what was happening to me. It made me stronger.

  * * *

Almost all teens who leave do it because they get to a point where they feel stronger and able to live without their abuser. They think about the future, and the kind of life they want to have, a life without abuse. And they feel hopeful that they can have that life. This is a new perspective, a new way of seeing themselves. And when they feel hopeful, they feel strong enough to leave, and build a new life without abuse.

Exercise

Use this blank page to write about your feelings or to make notes for yourself. What makes (or made) it difficult for you to leave your relationship if it is (or was) abusive?

11 What Can You Do if You Are Being Abused?

I never told anybody about it. Because I was ashamed. Now I can talk about it. Before, it hurt too bad, I didn't want to remember. I had nightmares about it. I tried to hide it from my mom. My mom and I are close, but there's some things that you can't talk about. But I figure from the very first time that he had hit me, if I had told my mom, there wouldn't have been another time—because he knew the consequences he'd have to face.

—Anonymous, 18

It made a difference to have the police and courts stop him. He came out of jail and we talked things out. He hasn't hit me since.

—Consuela, 19

[I finally attended a school in a different city.] Away from our abusive fights, I was able to build my self-reliance in small ways. I learned to have fun without Mike, to make decisions . . . and to [be okay without] seeing him every

day. Slowly, I built my self-confidence. I defined myself on my own terms, rather than seeing myself as Mike's girl-friend. . . . His own behavior also helped me break away from him. Although he started dating someone else, I still found it difficult to stay away from him. He became more and more violent. He smashed his fist through his new girl-friend's wall. I had believed until then that I was the only woman who could really "drive" him to violence.

—Marge, 19

I told my social worker at the health clinic. I told her because she always listened. She didn't blame me—for being pregnant or for him beating on me. It was a relief, because no one else believed it was happening. I told her because I was sick of it. But it was hard. It hurt a lot to talk about it. It made it real. But deep down inside, I was a really hurt person. When I told her, I believed it. What helped was a lot of counseling and a lot of friends telling me I was not a bad person. I had to hear it a lot of times, lots of times, but then I heard it.

—Felicia, 18

You deserve safety. You deserve love that doesn't hurt so much. You deserve to wake up every morning and feel free, not afraid.

You have a lot of strength. Remember the times you have been strong in dealing with being abused:

- Remember the times you said something or did something that kept you from being hurt worse.
- Remember the times you told someone about it.
- Remember the ways you have avoided the violence.

- Remember how you have kept going when you have felt so much fear and pain.

When you think about how you have survived the emotional pain and the physical injuries, are you surprised to realize how strong you are?

You can use your strength to plan for your safety and freedom from violence.

Look in a mirror. Say to yourself in the mirror, "I deserve to be loved without being hurt! I am strong and courageous! I am a survivor!"

Have your friends, your parents, and others all given you the same advice: "Get out! Break up with your abuser!"? This often happens to victims of abuse. People see the abuse, and don't understand the rest. They don't understand that you don't want the abuse, but you do want the love, and you do want the way it feels when it's good between you. Or they may not understand that you have been trying to break up, but it gets too scary, because he or she won't let you go.

When you saw the title of this section, **What Can You Do?**, did you say to yourself, "I know, they're going to say 'Break up with him (or her),' just like everyone else"?

As we said in the last section, this is a very difficult decision. The pull to be with your abuser and the urge to get away from him or her are both powerful. If you haven't decided yet whether to leave or to stay in the relationship, there are still things you can do to be safe and to protect yourself from the violence.

If you *have* decided to end the relationship, but have been afraid to do it, there are things you can do to be safe and to protect yourself from the violence while you are breaking up and afterward. You probably know by now that your abuser gets more violent when he or she believes that you are leaving him or her.

If you have broken up, there are things you can do to be safe, and to heal from the effects of the abuse.

Remember:

If you decide to leave, or

if you decide to stay, or

if you decide to think about it for a while longer, or

if you have already left,

you are strong, and you can be safe and protect yourself from violence.

Things You Can Do to Be Safe

How can you be safe? How can you cope? How can you begin to recover from the emotional and physical damage the abuse has caused you? How can you be free from the violence?

Take it seriously

Let your abuser know that emotional, sexual, and physical abuse are all *serious and dangerous.* You don't deserve it. Make it clear you won't allow it. If you insist that your abuser go for counseling or to Alcoholics Anonymous, or change his or her behavior, be ready to follow through on your threat or promise. If you say you'll leave if your abuser doesn't change, but you don't leave when the old behavior continues, the abuser will think he or she has your permission to continue the violence.

Plan for your safety

If you are *not* ready to break up, think of a safety plan for when your boyfriend or girlfriend is violent. If you *are* ready to break up, think of a safety plan for his or her explosive reaction or harassment to try to get you back. Think of whatever you can do to not be a target for the violence. For example, arrange for a safe place to stay. Arrange not to be alone at school, or on the way to and from school. *Include other people in your safety plan—your friends, your parents, sisters, brothers, neighbors, people at school.* If you have become isolated and alienated from your parents and other people in your life, remember that they can be helpful. You need support from adults for you to be safe.

Have someone else or a machine answer the telephone if you do not want to take your abuser's calls. If you are going out together, arrange to have a backup plan for getting home safely, and make sure someone knows where you are. Use what you know about your abuser's patterns and use all of your resources to come up with safety plans that will work for you.

Practice self-defense

There are many ways to make it clear to your abuser you won't allow violence. Planning for your own safety is one important way. You can let your abuser know loudly and clearly that you won't be hit, or that you won't have sex unless you want it. You can tell people about the abuser's violent behavior, rather than hiding it. You can take a self-defense class. Self-defense classes will teach you an attitude of strength and assertiveness, and how to deal with fear.

Use the legal system

Assaults, beatings, sexual coercion, rape—these are illegal. Your abuser's violence against you is a crime.

You can complain to authorities such as the police, your school administrators, or your dorm advisor if you are in college. Even if you are under eighteen, you can call the police. Violent boyfriends or girlfriends can be charged with:

Criminal harassment: subjecting you to physical contact, following you around, or phoning you continually if it is done to harass, alarm, or annoy you.

Reckless endangerment: placing you in serious fear of bodily injury or death.

Assault: intentionally or negligently causing or attempting to cause bodily injury.

Aggravated assault: intentionally or negligently causing or attempting to cause grave injury, as with a weapon.

Rape or attempted rape: sexual intercourse (penetration of the vagina) forced by violence or threat of violence.

Sexual assault: touching, rubbing, stroking, or using objects in a sex act forced by violence or the threat of violence. Also, touching, rubbing, or stroking by an adult of someone who is under eighteen.

Sodomy: forced penetration of the anus.

Forced oral sex: forcing you to give or receive oral sex.

You can get a *restraining order.* They are available to teens with help from an adult. A restraining order is an order by the court to the abuser to keep away from you. If the abuser violates the court order, he (or she) can be arrested. You file a request for a restraining order with a civil court. Call a nearby domestic violence hotline for information about how to get a restraining order in your area.

Tell an adult about the violence

Tell an adult about your experiences with violence. Begin by telling your parents. You need support to solve this problem, because you cannot handle it alone. Talking to friends can help you feel supported and not so alone. But you must also talk to adults. Other adult family members, besides your parents, may be good sources of support and help. At school, counselors, nurses, vice principals, principals, or teachers can help. Sometimes a coworker or a neighbor or a friend's parent can be helpful. *Find someone you can talk to.*

You may need to tell them more than once because they may not believe at first that you could be having such a serious problem. Or you might change your mind because when the violence stops for a while, you think it won't happen again. But keep telling them. If you have been in an abusive relationship for a while, your relationship with your parent or parents may be very complicated by now. Your parents may want to help, but not know how, or they may not understand your strong fears and feelings. Or your parents may be angry with you, or they may not be supportive of you in general. The first step is to try to get their support by telling them exactly what has happened, and why you are afraid of your abuser. If you have been sexually or emotionally abused, this may be difficult to explain. Tell them about specific incidents. You may show them this book, and sections that apply to your experience.

If you see a counselor first, plan with the counselor how to tell your parents. If your parents do not listen or help, you might feel hurt and angry. You might even feel that you are better off not confronting your abuse. But you must keep trying, and find an adult who will listen.

Call a hotline for information

Most cities have teen hotlines, domestic violence and rape hotlines, or crisis hotlines. There is a National Domestic Violence Hotline in the United States [(800) 799-7233]. It does not cost money to call this hotline number. Hotlines can help teens who are abusers, or who are afraid they will be abusers, as well as teens who have been abused. They can help gay teens as well as straight teens. They can also help friends and family members of someone who has a problem with dating violence.

You can find the phone number of local hotlines by looking in the telephone book under "teen" or "youth" or "rape" or "domestic violence" or "family violence" or "crisis." If you can't find it in the phone book, call information and tell the operator what you are looking for. The operator may know how it is listed.

Hotlines have trained counselors answering the phone. Some hotlines answer calls twenty-four hours a day, seven days a week. Others answer during certain hours, which you find out when you call. The hotline counselors can help you if you're upset and need someone to talk to. They can help if you have questions and need information. They can tell you how to find a counselor, or a legal service, or a support group near your home. They don't usually ask for your name, or they ask only for your first name, so you can feel safe that no one will know you or find out that you called.

Find a counselor or support group

Talking to a counselor or therapist who knows about dating violence can help you sort out your confused feelings

What to Do if You Are Being Abused:

- Take it seriously.
- Tell your abuser the violence must stop.
- Say it clearly if you don't want sex.
- Plan for your safety.
- Tell your parents or a trusted adult.
- Call the police or other authorities.
- Call a hotline.
- Find a counselor or a support group.
- Talk to friends.
- Do things for yourself that make you feel stronger.
- Take a self-defense class.

and become stronger in coping with the violence. Counseling can help you recover from the trauma you have experienced. A support group where you can talk with other girls or guys having the same or similar problems can help you so you don't feel so isolated and alone. You can learn from one another how to handle the problems that come up every day when you are in an abusive relationship, or when you have just ended one.

Your school counselor, your school nurse, a friend, a teen hotline, or a domestic violence hotline in your area may be able to suggest places to go for counseling. If your school has a counseling center, you might be able to find a counselor at your school.

Advice from Abused Teens

I would say once he hits you the first time, that is your chance to get out of the relationship. You should end it right there, because if you keep saying it's not going to happen again, you're going to keep repeatedly saying that. And pretty soon it's going to be too late.

—Anonymous, 18

Leave him alone altogether. If it means changing your phone number or relocating, do it.

—Don, 18

I want my education, to get a job. I have to learn different things so I don't get stuck. If he does it again, I know I'm not going to stay again. Now I'm thinking about my future. Maybe you don't leave him because you're scared of the guy or of his friends. Maybe you have no way out, no money, nowhere else to go. The main thing is to go to school. Get training. Be strong, talk to a friend or other people who have been abused.

—Consuela, 19

My advice to other girls is to tell the person who is hitting you or controlling you to stop it. Tell them, "If you don't like something I do, tell me. Let me be myself." I learned from being abused by my girlfriend, if you start hitting back, or hurting back, it gets worse. Don't let yourself get into that. If that person needs to go away, let her or him.

—Meybel, 19

I can look back on my relationship not with shame but with pride. I am proud of my own courage, which enabled me to grow strong. I am proud that I had the strength to say no to an abusive relationship. I can look back at my younger self and see in her the beginnings of a fighter, someone who would insist that she deserved something better than violence. I became someone who loves herself enough to settle for nothing less than happiness and self-respect.

—Marge, 18

Advice for Abused Girls from Abusive Guys Who Have Changed

Leave and find someone else. You don't need someone who's hitting you all the time.

—Paul, 18

I want to tell girls to get out of the relationship. Unless he becomes aware of the problem and wants to change, he won't change.

—Ruiz, 17

Call the police.

—Barry, 18

Keep away from him when he's going to rage at you. If he has to get out of the house or get away from you to cool off, let him go.

—Leonard, 16

I learned that a guy shouldn't want to have sex with a girl who doesn't want to. It isn't normal. If she's crying or begging him to stop or afraid of him, and he makes her do it anyway, that's sick. That is rape. I want to tell girls not to think that's normal.

—Albert, 17

Exercise

Use this blank page to write about your feelings or to make notes for yourself. Think about a plan of action for yourself.

12 What Can You Do if You Are Abusive?

I was sure I'd never hit a girl because my dad beat my mom. But I felt I had to have control, and I did. I had a hard time trusting girls. I used to hit [my girlfriend], punch her, slap her. I told her she was no good and called her a slut. I choked her and threatened to kill her. Now I am working on my issues in counseling. I have learned to talk to [my girlfriend] and use a time-out when I am angry. I now can look at what she is going through.

—Paul, 18

I emotionally abused her by telling her one thing and doing the opposite. I controlled her dress, behavior, and who she could be friends with. I used my gang to intimidate her by pointing out victims and threatening to do the same to her. Now I think about negative consequences for assault, like jail. I also think about how it affects her.

—Ruiz, 17

I f you have a problem with violent behavior, if you are emotionally or sexually abusive, you must find ways to change your behavior so that you don't hurt someone you care about. In the long run, you are hurting yourself.

You *can* control your anger so that you don't hurt anyone. No matter what anyone else does, you have the choice to act in a way that is not violent. You have the choice to act with self-respect and respect for others.

It is illegal to harass or assault someone, including someone you are in a relationship with. There are serious consequences for harassing, assaulting, or sexually assaulting someone. You can be kicked out of school. You can be arrested. You can go to jail.

You *Can* Stop the Violence
How can you keep yourself from being violent?

Acknowledge that you have a problem
The first step in overcoming a problem with violence is to say to yourself and to others, "I have a problem. I don't want to be abusive." If you feel that you want to control your violence so that your girlfriend won't leave you, then that is a beginning.

But you have to want it for yourself, whether your girlfriend leaves or stays. It is hard to change. It takes a lot of courage. You need a vision of yourself in the future: calm, secure, able to control yourself, accepting of yourself, and not blaming others for your problems. You need a sense deep inside you that you know you can be different, and that you can make your life better.

Make a commitment to yourself: I will not hit. I will not force or coerce sex. I will not emotionally attack or manipulate.

Find a counselor or support group

Counseling can help you understand your problems and your feelings. Counseling can help you learn ways to handle your anger without hurting anyone. You can learn to recognize your own behavior patterns. Then you can find ways to stop yourself before you lose control. You can learn empathy for your girlfriend or boyfriend, to understand how she or he feels when you treat her or him badly. You can learn about healthy sex and love.

Counseling can help you find out about your feelings and why you react the way that you do.

If you join a group with others who have the same problem, you can learn how others deal with relationships. You can get support from other guys to find new ways to act with girls, and new ways to cope with frustration, stress, and anger.

Join Alcoholics Anonymous or a drug program

If you are abusing drugs or alcohol, then you are not dealing with your problem with violence. If your excuse for being violent is that you were drunk, then you have to stop drinking and deal directly with your violence. Take responsibility for it. When you are sober or clean, you can seriously say to yourself, *I have a problem to solve.* And you can start the process of solving your problems rather than escaping from them.

Educate yourself

Read about relationship violence, about people who have overcome it, about how it affects its victims. Talk to others about it. Watch television shows and movies about it. Learn as much as you can to understand your experiences.

Confronting your violence means changing your attitudes toward women in general, and toward victims, and developing respect for them. It means changing your attitudes about violence, until you believe that it is not acceptable.

Advice from Abusive Guys Who Have Changed

Try and get help. Join violent offender groups. Stop and think before something happens that could ruin your or someone else's life. Don't deny emotions.

—Allen, 18

A "real man" respects and pleases a girl during sex. A "real man" doesn't want to force or trick a girl to do it. Think about it—are you a "real man"?

—Barry, 18

Look at what you're doing to your girlfriend, and put yourself in her shoes. How would you like it?

—Paul, 18

Nobody controls you. You can control yourself. You make your own choices. It's not okay to retaliate.

—Ray, 18

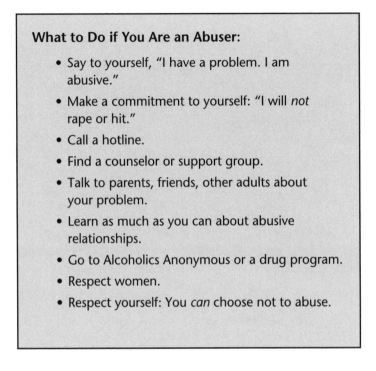

What to Do if You Are an Abuser:

- Say to yourself, "I have a problem. I am abusive."
- Make a commitment to yourself: "I will *not* rape or hit."
- Call a hotline.
- Find a counselor or support group.
- Talk to parents, friends, other adults about your problem.
- Learn as much as you can about abusive relationships.
- Go to Alcoholics Anonymous or a drug program.
- Respect women.
- Respect yourself: You *can* choose not to abuse.

Think of the consequences.

—David, 17

It's a cycle beginning with verbal abuse and turns into physical abuse against people you care for.

—Steve, 20

Walk away before things get heated up. If you can't do that, you should get help. It's not right to hit girls.

—Gilbert, 17

Exercise

Use this blank page to write about your feelings or to make notes for yourself. Think about a plan of action for yourself to deal with this problem.

13 What Can You Do if Your Friend Is in an Abusive Relationship?

I was there and he got real mad. First he started screaming at her and calling her names. Then he shoved her into the car and started slapping her. She was scared and tried to tell him that she loved him. I got mad and yelled at him to stop, that she didn't do anything wrong. My boyfriend also tried to get him to stop. He put his hand on his arm and told him to calm down, that this was no way to treat a girlfriend. Later, we talked with her and kept telling her he had no right to hit her.

—Mercedes, 19

At first I tried to tell him to leave, but he didn't want to hear about it. I didn't know what to do. So I was just there for him.

—Roy, 18

My friend came running over to help me. If it hadn't been for her, I might be dead. He kept trying to smother me. . . . My friend got me to the school—and said that if I didn't press charges, she would.

—Salina, 13

If you have a friend who is being victimized in an abusive relationship, what can you do?

Help your friend recognize the abuse

Ask questions and talk about what is happening to her or him. Help your friend to see that what is happening is not normal and to see the signs of abuse. Tell her or him that it will probably get worse.

Support your friend's strength

Recognize the things that your friend does to take care of herself or himself. Encourage your friend's strength and courage. Encourage your friend to do things with you, and with other friends, to have some enjoyment apart from the relationship.

Be nonjudgmental

Try to see that your friend is confused because she or he is frightened by the violence, but wants the love or security from being with the boyfriend or girlfriend. If your friend wants to stay in the relationship, or goes back and forth about it, try not to say that it is wrong. Tell your friend that you are worried about her or his safety and self-respect. Help your friend see that she or he is not to blame for the violence. Help your friend recognize the abuser's excuses for being violent (which blame the victim).

Help your friend with safety plans

Help your friend focus on being safe. Help your friend use what she or he knows about particular resources and about the abuser's patterns to figure out ways to be safe when the abuser is explosive or violent, or verbally or sexually abusive. For example, if your friend is a girl who is being abused or harassed by her boyfriend, walk with her to school or have her stay over at your house when he is threatening her.

Be there to listen
Even if your friend breaks up with the abuser and then goes back, listen. Be supportive. Eventually your friend will leave, especially with the support of friends.

If your friend breaks up with the abuser, keep up the support
It takes a while to get over a relationship that is violent. Keep in close contact through the times your friend feels lonely, or scared, or bad about herself or himself. Your friend may feel like getting back together. She or he may miss the boyfriend or girlfriend, or may not feel strong enough to resist the pressure to get back together.

Help your friend talk to adults to get help
Talk with your friend about telling parents or other adults. Go with her or him to see a counselor or to enroll in a support group. If she or he won't talk to an adult, then *you must find an adult you trust to talk to* about it. Ask your parents or a school counselor, nurse, or administrator. Ask the adult to help, to reach out, to intervene. Talk to your friend's parents about what is happening. Don't assume that your friend's parents know about the abuse.

If you become frightened or frustrated, get support from friends and family members or other adults

Educate yourself about dating violence. *You can't rescue your friend.* You can't neglect your own life to take care of her or him. But with support for yourself, you can calmly hang in there and support your friend as she or he goes through the ups and downs of dealing with the violence.

14 You Can Have a Healthy Relationship

After breaking up with Andy, . . . I [gradually] became more relaxed, and I wasn't afraid to say what I wanted to anyone anymore. [My new boyfriend] holds me when I get upset and lets me cry. Never does he put me down or even come close to hitting me. We can argue. He is so patient.

—Anonymous, 14

In healthy relationships, young men and women make decisions thoughtfully together and communicate with each other. When they disagree, they argue and discuss their differences. They listen to each other's viewpoints and feelings. When they have a conflict, they negotiate. They find a way to compromise so that they can both get what they need. When one of them gets angry or loses his or her temper, that person can calm down so he or she won't become violent. For example, Linda said:

I got so upset when John insisted that I come over to his house for Christmas. We were so mad at each other. I wanted to be with him, but I wanted to be with my family. We talked

and finally worked it out together. We spent Christmas Eve
with my family and Christmas Day with his.

If one person feels hurt by the other, they can talk about
it. They can apologize without feeling humiliated or afraid.
If one feels like having time alone, or wants to do things
separately, the other can accept it. Thomas said:

Right after school, or sometimes when I lose my temper, I
just want to watch TV by myself, you know, to chill out.
On the days when I go home from school with Judy, I have
to explain, "I'll see ya later." Usually she wants to hang
out with me right after school, but she gets it. I'll be bet-
ter to hang out with later. We don't get jealous or anything
like that.

If either one of them approaches the other to have sex
and the other one doesn't want to, they talk about it, and
stop. Or they talk about it and change what they were doing
so that both of them are comfortable. Both feel free to stop
at any time during sex. Josh said:

When my girlfriend started crying and said she just
couldn't go down on me, I held her and said we didn't
have to unless she wanted to.

They trust that the other person will understand. They
are careful to discuss how to protect themselves from AIDS
and pregnancy. They feel respected and cared for.

They have fun together and they are free to enjoy themselves. They are not afraid that they will be cruelly hurt if

they say or do something that their boyfriend or girlfriend thinks is wrong. Valerie said:

I didn't know what to do. I knew I'd be late, but I couldn't reach Lisa to tell her. I thought she'd be so mad, and I was scared because of how my last girlfriend used to attack me over every little thing. Lisa was mad, and worried, and she told me how mad she was. But she also listened and believed me when I explained what happened. It was over in a minute!

There is no room for fear in a healthy relationship. Each person trusts the other. They can enjoy each other's successes at school, in sports, or in other activities. They can enjoy that their girlfriend or boyfriend has lots of friends and interests and dreams for the future. Trudy said:

I told my boyfriend, James, about this guy in my class who works at this place where I just got a job. The guy told me all about the place, so now I'm not so nervous. James said I was lucky to know someone already.

They do not try to restrict or control one another. They do not keep their girlfriend or boyfriend from doing things because of their own fears. They encourage and support one another. Selma said:

You know what I like best about Tony? He's on my team. It's going to be hard to get through all the years of college I have ahead of me. He cheers me on every step of the way! We do that for each other.

Exercise

Use this blank page to write about your feelings or to make notes for yourself. Write about what it would be like to be in a healthy relationship.

AFTERWORD TO THE NEW EDITION:
Advice for Parents

When you first discover that your teenager has been beaten up by a boyfriend or girlfriend, or sexually or emotionally abused, you will have the urge to take dramatic steps to get the abuser out of your teen's life. You will feel outraged and fearful for your teen's safety, and you will want to protect her or him immediately. Ideally, you can do that. But immediate, dramatic steps to get the victim away from the abuser only work when the victim is ready to participate in getting away.

In some of the examples below, I refer to the victim as female and the abuser as male (the most common scenario statistically), but abusers and victims may be male or female, in same-sex or heterosexual relationships.

Parents usually have several priorities, all of them high, competing for their attention at once. On reflection, you may realize that you have several goals. You want your teen to

- end the battering and the battering relationship,
- be as safe as possible, and to take care of his or her safety,

- become free of the hold the abuser has over him or her,
- stop the violence and threats that frighten all of you,
- stop the damaging effect this has on your family life,
- and heal and recover.

There are many ways you can be effective in dealing with the abuse even if your teen can't or won't end the relationship. As you try to find ways to help, you do not want to cut off contact with your teen, which will leave her or him more isolated and vulnerable.

You must be direct and clear about the danger your daughter is in and the damage the relationship is causing her. You want to set limits while keeping a strong connection with her. But do so without accusing, excessively criticizing, punishing or restricting, or trying to control her. You will lose the battle if she feels controlled by both her boyfriend and by you, leaving her with no safe way to think for herself. Imagine the effect on her if you police her activities or criticize her—and her abusive boyfriend does the same thing.

As parents, we can't control our teenage children, but we can influence them and be resources for them. You can disengage from power struggles, telling yourself to detach and listen. When tension is building between you and your teen, listen calmly, clarify what's being said or felt, and respond thoughtfully.

You must help your daughter build strengths in all aspects of her life so that she can be as strong as possible to resist the intensity of her relationship with her boyfriend. Support, do not ignore, the aspects of her life that are working well in spite of the abuse. Engage her family, friends, neighbors, and people at school in ways they can all support and look out for her. Strengthen your relationship with her. Maintaining open communication may give your teen a lifeline that keeps her safe.

The values and beliefs of your culture or your religion may affect your feelings and your family's response to your daughter's abusive relationship. Sometimes these cultural influences are barriers to a family's effectiveness in helping an abused teen, because they can limit your understanding or your options for helping. Other times, these cultural traditions provide supportive resources to the family. It is important to challenge beliefs that get in the way of protecting your daughter's safety. When you actively intervene on your daughter's behalf, she knows that she has the right to be treated with respect, that she doesn't deserve to be abused, and that abuse is never acceptable—in any culture. The support that is available within your culture can be helpful and empowering and strengthen your daughter's ties to her family and community, diminishing the control the abuser has over her.

A teen's abusive relationship can put every member of the family on an emotional roller coaster. Your daughter has probably gone back and forth, breaking up and getting back together with her boyfriend—feeling close with him when he is not being abusive, breaking up after a violent incident, then getting back together when he apologizes and they make up. As her relationship with her boyfriend goes back and forth, so does her relationship with you. Communication between parents and other family members may be difficult when you are so focused on your child's dramatic changes.

Victor, whose daughter was in an abusive relationship, describes a turning point in his family's ability to understand and protect their daughter and the family from the chaos caused by her relationship:

We couldn't keep Emilia under lock and key, and her ups and downs were consuming us. . . . We had to slow down and get our minds off this. Rosa and I talked. We decided that every week we were going to do something as a family and as a couple. We took time out to talk with both our daughters more. We were determined to have fun again. We went to the movies, and sometimes Emilia would come with us and enjoy herself.

Emilia was able to leave her boyfriend with the support of her family. Help your daughter use her strengths to plan for her safety, to plan to end the relationship, or, if she's not going to end it, to take care of herself while she is in it. She knows the abuser and his patterns better than anyone, so she can determine the safest ways to leave or to protect herself. She may not realize until she reads this book or until you help her see that there are ways to be safe whether she stays or leaves. When breaking up, the major concern is avoiding contact with the abuser, who may be volatile. Safety planning focuses on her staying away from him, and on keeping him away from her.

Many people leaving an abusive relationship are vulnerable to going back, especially when they feel drawn back to the emotional intensity or by the desperate suffering of the abuser. Don't assume that your teen's need for your support is over because the relationship is over. Your teen needs continuous support, and will likely be emotionally vulnerable and/or in physical danger for a long time after the breakup. She needs help to overcome the fear, isolation, and damaged self-esteem she experienced during the relationship. She may need counseling to recover from the effects of the trauma she has been through.

In spite of the heartbreak and pain, teens recover and families are resilient. Your resilience enables you to draw upon your reserves to find the strength and the capability to handle one of the most difficult problems a parent can face.

Safety Planning

Your safety is the most important thing. Listed below are tips to help keep you safe. After you read them, make a safety plan that works for you.

If you are dating someone, think about . . .

- double-dating the first few times you go out with a new person.
- before leaving on a date, knowing the exact plans for the evening and making sure a parent or friend knows these plans and what time to expect you home. Let your date know that you are expected to call or tell that person when you get in.
- being aware of your decreased ability to react under the influence of alcohol or drugs.
- if you leave a party with someone you do not know well, making sure you tell another person you are leaving and with whom. Ask a friend to call and make sure you arrived home safely.
- asserting yourself when necessary. Be firm and straightforward in your relationships.
- trusting your instincts. If a situation makes you uncomfortable, try to be calm and think of a way to remove yourself from the situation.

Adapted from the following sources: Oakland County Coordinating Council against Domestic Violence (www.domesticviolence.org), Metro Nashville Police Department's personalized safety plan, Domestic Violence Advocacy Program of Family Resources, Inc. Safety Planning Worksheet.

If you are in an abusive relationship, think about . . .

- keeping important phone numbers nearby. Numbers to have besides your parents' numbers are those of the police, hotlines, other family members, and friends.

- friends or neighbors you could tell about the abuse. Ask them to call the police if they see anything suspicious or hear angry or violent noises. Make up a code word that you can use when you need help.

- how to get out of your home or wherever you spend time with your partner safely. Practice ways to get out.

- safer places in your home where there are exits and no weapons. If you feel abuse is going to happen, try to get your abuser to one of these.

- ways that you could get any weapons out of the house.

- where you could go to be safe, even if you do not plan to break up. Think of how you might get there. Put together a bag of things you use every day (see the checklist on page 119). Hide it where it is easy for you to get.

- going over your safety plan often.

If you consider leaving your abuser, think about . . .

- four places you could go if it isn't safe for you to stay at home.

- people who might help you if you leave, who will keep a bag for you, who might lend you money, and who will spend time with you.

- keeping change for phone calls or getting a cell phone.

- how you might leave and go about breaking up. Practice how you would leave or break up safely.

- if you have children, how you can take them with you safely. There are times when taking your children with you may put all of your lives in danger. You need to protect yourself first in order to be able to protect your children.

- what you will need to take with you if you leave:

ITEMS TO TAKE, IF POSSIBLE

Driver's license
Money
Keys to car, house, work
Welfare identification
Extra clothes
Medicine
Important papers for you and your children:
>   Birth certificates
>   Social security cards
>   School and medical records
>   Insurance papers
>   Bankbooks, credit cards
>   Address book
>   Passports, green cards, work permits
>   Car registration

Other items:

Lease/rental agreement
Mortgage payment book, unpaid bills
Protective Order (PO), divorce papers, custody orders
Pictures, jewelry, things that mean a lot to you
Items for your children (toys, blankets, etc.)

If you have left your abuser, think about . . .

- your safety—you still need to.
- getting a cell phone and programming it to call 911.
- getting a Protective Order (PO) from the court. Keep a copy with you all the time. Give a copy to the police,

people who take care of your children, your school, and your boss.

- changing the locks. Consider putting in stronger doors, smoke and carbon monoxide detectors, a security system, and outside lights.

- telling friends and neighbors that you are no longer with your abuser. Ask them to call the police if they see your abuser near your home.

- telling people who take care of your children the names of people who are allowed to pick them up. If you have a PO protecting your children, give their teachers and babysitters a copy of it.

- telling someone at work and/or school about what has happened. Ask that person to screen your calls. If you have a PO that includes school or work, consider giving the principal or your boss a copy of it and a picture of the abuser. Think about and practice a safety plan for your school or workplace. This should include going to and from school or work.

- not going to the same hangouts or stores you did when you were with your abuser.

- someone who you can call if you feel down or lonely. Also think about going to a support group or workshop.

- a safe way to speak with your abuser if you must.

- going over your safety plan often.

WARNING: Abusers try to control their victims' lives. When abusers feel a loss of control—like when victims try to leave them—the abuse often gets worse. Take special care when you leave, and after you have left.

YOUR SAFETY PLAN WORKSHEET

Increasing safety in the relationship:

✗ *I will have important phone numbers and change for phone calls with me at all times.*

Important phone numbers:

Police _____

Hotline _____

Friends _____

_____

Family _____

_____

_____

_____

✗ *I can tell* _____ *and* _____ *about the violence and ask them to call the police if they hear or see anything that leads them to suspect I might be in danger.*

✗ *I can alert* _____ *and* _____ *at school, work, etc. that I might need to ask them to help me be safe.*

✗ *If I have to get away from the person who is violent toward me, I can go to (list four places you can go to be safe):*

_____

_____

_____

_____

✗ I can leave money, car keys, and _____
_____ with
_____ so I can get
to them in an emergency.

Increasing safety when the relationship is over:
✗ I can tell _____ and
_____ at school/work/
other about my situation and ask them to screen
my calls/visitors, etc.

✗ I can alert neighbors _____
and _____ to let me
know if they see anyone stalking me or prowling.

✗ I can obtain a protective order and keep it with or
near me at all times as well as leave a copy with
_____

✗ I will talk to _____
and _____ and
_____ about my need
for support when I feel frightened or don't think I
can successfully keep my ex away from me or keep
myself away from my ex.

✗ I can go to stay with _____
or _____ if I
have to be safe.

✗ If I feel down, I can call _____
or _____ for support, or
attend workshops and support groups to strengthen
my relationships with other people.

Resources

Hotlines

Childhelp
(800) 4-A-CHILD [(800) 422-4453]
www.childhelpusa.org
Offers crisis intervention and local referrals.

National Domestic Violence Hotline
(800) 799-SAFE [(800) 799-7233]
(800) 787-3224 TTY
www.ndvh.org/educate/teen.html
A twenty-four-hour hotline for victims and anyone calling on their behalf. Provides crisis intervention, safety planning, and referrals to agencies in all fifty states, Puerto Rico, and the U.S. Virgin Islands. In English and Spanish, with interpreters available for most languages. See website for information on teens and dating violence.

National Organization for Victim Assistance
(800) TRY-NOVA [(800) 879-6682]
A twenty-four-hour hotline for victims of crime and crisis everywhere. Provides information and referrals for victims of crime and disaster.

National STD/HIV Hotline
(800) 227-8922
Anonymous, confidential, and reliable answers to questions about sexually transmitted diseases and HIV/AIDS.

Rape, Abuse, and Incest National Network
(800) 656-HOPE [(800) 656-4673]
www.rainn.org
Free and confidential twenty-four-hour hotline from the largest anti-sexual assault organization in the nation. Beginning in fall 2006, RAINN will launch a web-based hotline service. Website provides referrals and tips on preventing and dealing with sexual assault.

Youth Crisis Hotline
(800) HIT-HOME [(800) 448-4663]
Provides intervention for teens in crisis situations.

Books

Bancroft, Lundy. *Why Does He Do That?: Inside the Minds of Angry and Controlling Men.* New York: Putnam's Sons, 2002. From a former codirector of Emerge, the first U.S. program for abusive men, this book explores why men abuse.

Crompton, Vicki, and Ellen Zelda Kessner. *Saving Beauty from the Beast: How to Protect Your Daughter from an Unhealthy Relationship.* Boston: Little, Brown & Company, 2004. This book offers specific advice for parents on talking about and confronting teen dating violence.

Gaddis, Patricia Riddle. *Dangerous Dating: Helping Young Women Say No to Abusive Relationships.* Colorado Springs, CO: Shaw, 2000. Advice for parents and counselors on helping young women deal with abusive dating situations.

Jones, Ann, and Susan Schechter. *When Love Goes Wrong: What to Do When You Can't Do Anything Right.* New York: HarperCollins, 1993. Provides guidance and practical options for women in controlling and emotionally abusive relationships.

Levy, Barrie, and Patricia Occhiuzzo Giggans. *What Parents Need to Know about Dating Violence.* Seattle: Seal Press, 1995. Drawing on the real-life experiences of parents and teens as well as on their own professional experience, the authors offer straightforward advice for parents who are concerned with teenagers in abusive relationships.

McGee, Kathleen, and Laura Buddenberg. *Unmasking Sexual Con Games: Teen Guide.* Boys Town, NE: Boys Town Press, 2003. Tips that help teens create healthy sexual boundaries and protect themselves from being intimidated or conned into sex.

Miles, Al. *Ending Violence in Teen Dating Relationships: A Resource Guide for Parents and Pastors.* Minneapolis: Augsburg Books, 2005. Critical information that parents, caregivers, clergy, and educators can use to protect teens and help them foster healthy dating relationships.

Murray, Jill. *But I Love Him: Protecting Your Teen Daughter from Controlling, Abusive Dating Relationships.* New York: Regan Books, 2001. Murray shows parents how to help their teens escape from physically and emotionally abusive relationships.

Peter, Val J., and Ronald W. Herron. *What's Right for Me?: Making Good Choices in Relationships.* Boys Town, NE: Boys Town Press, 1998. Prepares teens for situations and people who may be negative influences while emphasizing talking to adults about threatening situations.

Pledge, Deanna S. *When Something Feels Wrong: A Survival Guide about Abuse, for Young People.* Minneapolis: Free Spirit Publishing, 2002. This book provides creative and pragmatic ways of dealing with abuse and getting help.

Rue, Nancy, and Rudolf Steiner. *Everything You Need to Know about Abusive Relationships.* New York: Rosen Publishing Group, 1998. Discusses different kinds of abuse that occur between teens who are dating and offers advice on how to handle abusive situations.

Warshaw, Robin. *I Never Called It Rape: The Ms. Report on Recognizing, Fighting, and Surviving Date and Acquaintance Rape.* New York: Harper and Row, 1994. Discusses the *Ms. Magazine* Campus Project on Sexual Assault. Includes many statistics, clear definitions, and firsthand accounts.

Organizations and Websites

For Teens:

The Body: Safer Sex Guides & Information
http://thebody.com/safesex/safer.html
This website is dedicated to safe sex information for teens.

Break the Cycle
(310) 286-3366
(888) 988-TEEN [(888) 988-8336]
www.breakthecycle.org
Empowers youth to end domestic violence.

Campaign for Our Children
www.cfoc.org/411aboutsex/safedatingforteens/
Provides safe dating tips for teens, plus information on birth control, drugs and sex, STDs, and sexual violence.

Cool Nurse
www.coolnurse.com/teen_dating_violence.htm
Tips for teens on identifying and understanding dating violence.

Covenant House
(800) 999-9999
460 W. 41st St.
New York, NY 10036
www.covenanthouse.org
In its locations across and outside of the United States, Covenant House provides shelter and services for homeless and runaway youth. The hot-line provides international crisis intervention for youth.

Dating Violence
www.acadv.org/dating.html
This website provides checklists for teens who think they might be in abusive relationships. It also lists a "Dating Bill of Rights" outlining teens' rights and responsibilities to themselves in relationships.

Dating Violence
www.intheknowzone.com/dating_violence
This website provides an overview of abusive behavior in relationships, and tips for helping abused friends.

GirlsAllowed

www.girlsallowed.org

This animated website tells the stories of Anni, her friends, and her boyfriends. Geared toward younger teenagers and kids.

I Wanna Know

www.iwannaknow.org

This site, sponsored by the American Social Health Association, provides facts and other information on teen sexual health and sexually transmitted diseases.

National Youth Violence Prevention Resource Center

www.safeyouth.org/scripts/teens/dating.asp

Provides information on teen dating violence, including a useful fact sheet.

Promote Truth

www.promotetruth.org

Promote Truth is a website for teens who want to learn more about sexual violence and dating. Includes sections for victims and survivors, parents and teachers, and professionals who work with teens. There is also a message board for users who want to talk with other teens and share their stories.

Scarleteen

www.scarleteen.com

This is an easy-to-use website covering the latest and most important issues concerning sex education, relationships, and the teen years.

See It and Stop It

www.seeitandstopit.org

This website is for teens who have friends who are in abusive relationships. It gives advice on how to step in and stop abusive behaviors and talk to both abusers and victims.

Teen Central

www.teencentral.net

Offers an anonymous web-based helpline, professionally monitored teen discussions, and many other resources.

Teen Relationships Website
(650) 312-8515
http://teenrelationships.org/
This site is for teens in relationships who want to learn more about abuse and how to create healthy, respectful relationships. It also gives advice on how to help friends. Website chat room on Mon.–Wed., 5:00–7:00 PM Pacific time.

TeenWire
www.teenwire.com
This is Planned Parenthood's website for teens, loaded with information about sexuality and relationships.

U Have the Right
www.uhavetheright.net
A website to help teens with building healthy relationships and understanding dating violence.

When Love Hurts
www.dvirc.org.au/whenlove/
A guide for teens on love, respect, and abuse in relationships.

WomensLaw.org
www.womenslaw.org/teens.htm
This website provides general information for teens who are being abused and offers a legal perspective.

For Parents:

CyberParent
www.cyberparent.com/abuse
Links to short articles for parents on verbal, emotional, and physical abuse, and teens who batter.

Family Education
http://life.familyeducation.com/dating/violence/34409.html
Useful tips for parents who are trying to talk to their kids about dating, relationships, and sex.

Family Violence Prevention Fund
http://endabuse.org/
Offers resources, links, and research.

Love Is Not Abuse
www.loveisnotabuse.com
A valuable site that provides a number of free downloadable handbooks on dating violence for both teens and parents. Click on "just for teens" for information and guidance geared toward young people.

National Center for Victims of Crime: Teen Victim Project
www.ncvc.org/tvp
Parents and people who work with teens can download a number of useful fact sheets, and can download or order a free hard copy of a new guide for victim service providers, Reaching and Serving Teen Victims: A Practical Handbook.

National Coalition against Domestic Violence
(303) 839-1852
1120 Lincoln Street
Denver, CO 80203
http://ncadv.org/
Under the "Protect Yourself" heading, there is valuable information on getting help and tips on Internet safety. You can also purchase a helpful Teen Dating Violence Resource Manual *through the website.*

National Council on Child Abuse and Family Violence
(202) 429-6695
1025 Connecticut Ave. NW, Ste. 1000
Washington, DC 20036
http://nccafv.org

Acknowledgments

Thank you to the people of all ages who, dedicated to helping teens have violence-free relationships, have helped make this book possible. It has been a pleasure to work with Denise Silva at Avalon Publishing/ Seal Press. Thank you, Denise, for your wonderful research and editorial skills. A special thank you to Faith Conlon, whose leadership at Seal Press and commitment to educating women and girls through books to prevent domestic violence led me to write this and my other books.

Linda Fischer and others at Project PAVE in Denver encouraged young men to share their experiences as abusers. Ruth Beaglehole at the Business Industry School in Los Angeles involved her students in reviewing the manuscript, and provided priceless feedback at crucial stages in writing this book. Linda's and Ruth's enthusiasm and dedication to youth are inspirational.

Many girls and parents spent hours telling their stories and reliving their nightmares to prevent other girls and parents from having to go through the kinds of violence they experienced. The girls and social workers who wrote their stories in *Dating Violence: Young Women in Danger* contributed again to educating young women and men about the realities of dating violence.

Patti Giggans, my coauthor of *What Parents Need to Know about Dating Violence,* contributed her insights and wide-ranging expertise to the Afterword for parents.

Sheila Kuehl provided legal information, and Ginny NiCarthy provided material for the section on addictive love—both from their contributions to *Dating Violence: Young Women in Danger.*

I have a wonderful cheering squad: I am indebted to my daughter, Johanna, for her review and suggestions about the original manuscript, and to Linda Garnets, for brainstorming, support, and inspiration.

ABOUT THE AUTHOR

Barrie Levy, M.S.W., is on the faculty of two UCLA departments: Social Welfare and Women's Studies. She is consultant to the Westside Domestic Violence Network and a psychotherapist in private practice. She is a nationally recognized trainer on adult and adolescent domestic and sexual violence. She has appeared on over fifteen television shows and written many books and articles, including *Skills for Violence-Free Relationships* (a curriculum for high school students), *Dating Violence: Young Women in Danger,* and *What Parents Need to Know about Dating Violence.* During thirty years in this field, she has founded and directed four domestic violence organizations.

Selected Titles from Seal Press

For more than thirty years, Seal Press has published ground-breaking books. By women. For women. Visit our website at www.sealpress.com.

Pissed Off: On Women and Anger by Spike Gillespie. $14.95, 1-58005-162-6. An amped up and personal self-help book that encourages women to go ahead and use that middle finger without being closed off to the notion of forgiveness.

You Can Be Free: An Easy-to-Read Handbook for Abused Women by Ginny NiCarthy and Sue Davidson. $13.95, 1-58005-159-6. In this bestselling guide, the authors take practical and gentle guidance to help women work toward building relationships that are healthier and, most importantly, safer.

Helping Her Get Free: A Guide for Families and Friends of Abused Women by Susan Brewster. $13.95, 1-58005-167. This straightforward and compassionate book offers the information needed to help give strength to women who are trying to break free.

Invisible Girls: The Truth About Sexual Abuse by Patti Feuereisen with Caroline Pincus. $15.95, 1-5800-135-9. An incredibly important and one-of-a-kind resource specifically for girls and young women who have suffered sexual abuse.

Solo: On Her Own Adventure edited by Susan Fox Rogers. $15.95, 1-58005-137-5. An inspiring collection of travel narratives that reveal the complexities of women journeying alone.

A Matter of Choice: 25 People Who Have Transformed Their Lives edited by Joan Chatfield-Taylor. $14.95, 1-58005-118-9. An inspiring collection of essays by people who made profound changes in their work, personal life, location, or lifestyle, proving that it is indeed never too late to take the road less traveled.